The Wallygrange Grammar School Blog!
Mike Knowles

About this Book

Please allow me to introduce myself, gentle reader!
I am Alfred Scholar, NUT TA.
You haven't heard of me? But how can that be possible?
Come on! *Think!*

I'm the headmaster the magazine *"Teaching Today,"* described as: *"...a man literally basking in the white hot heat of cutting edge education!"* Or they would have done if they'd accepted the bribe I offered them. What fools! But it was their loss and my gain. They lost the chance of an award winning article on the greatest teacher since...oh, I don't know. Think of some great teachers. And *I* gained back the money I would have spent bribing them. Simple logic. But let's not ponder any further on this bunch of fifth rate magazine hacks. Hacks who, when offered a wad of notes that would choke a Hippopotamus, chose instead to turn a blind eye. Or, to be more exact, an empty wallet!

You have an insatiable interest in all things educational. Am I right? Of course I am. Otherwise you wouldn't be reading this. And you certainly won't be disappointed because I'm about to allow you a glimpse of the fabled Seventh Heaven of Academia. In my book I will demonstrate beyond *any* possible doubt whatsoever that Wallygrange Grammar School has achieved what those so-called experts in the field of education have been singularly unable to do. And, whilst their efforts have fallen on stony ground, ours have flourished beyond all expectations. And why have they flourished? They've flourished because they've been cocooned within a rich compost. A *mental* compost. A compost that has been fermenting away within my brain. Even now green shoots are emerging with a velocity just short of the speed of light. Emerging and blossoming into fruition in the blink of an eye. This book describes in an astonishingly innovative way the happy and prosperous marriage betwixt Information Technology and the tried and tested methods of secondary education. A marriage that can only continue to flourish as time goes on and is destined to bear many equally and incredibly innovative offspring from between its glistening loins.

And, if all this should sound modest, then that's because it's meant to be. For I'm not one to exaggerate my accomplishments.

Warning! Some Important Legal and Other Notifications

You see how clever I've been? By allowing the metaphors to flow like wine I'll wager you're now be in an unseemly haste to get to the meat of my book. You are, aren't you? I thought so. And I can fully understand that. Especially when a book promises to deliver as much as mine undoubtedly does. But I urge you to be patient! The publishers and I cannot over-emphasize how important it is that you do *not* skip this section. Even if your temptation matches that of a crack addict! *Fight it with all your might! Fight it with every sinew within your body!* We beg you on bended knees! Go Cold Turkey until you've read the whole of this section. Unless, of course, you suffer from an Attention Deficit Disorder. In which case you may not have even got this far.

Thank you.

Alfred Scholar NUT TA.

Headmaster Wallygrange Grammar School.

Legal Notification!

This affidavit, which has been composed *a fortiori* by the greatest minds the legal profession can currently come up with, categorically state that "*Wheek Gooseberry Wine*" is a trademark of the Wheek International Gooseberry Wine Company. And will remain so *ad infinitum* or beyond. The affidavit also states that whilst the word "*gooseberry*" can be used on its own, let it be now and forever known that using it with the word "wine" will represent an infringement of copyright. Finally, please note that the plaintiff, one Ian Wheek, has a whole gang of sharp eyed lawyers just waiting to catch someone using those words without his permission. You wouldn't steal a horse, would you? You wouldn't steal a loaf of bread? So don't steal those words. They belong to us and to no one else.

I. Wheek. CEO Wheek International Gooseberry Wine Company.

DISCLAIMER!

The Author would like to stress that any resemblances to the prestigious King's School in Macclesfield are purely coincidental. We're not like them and we never will be. So please don't think we are. Wallygrange Grammar School, (motto: *Quis Paget Entrat**), is situated in the delightful village of Prestbury and is, by a happy coincidence, located right next to the sewage works.**

Who pays gets in. (Note that this may – and probably is – the same as the motto of a fictitious public school created by the satirical magazine Private Eye. *However, this must not be mistaken for plagiarism. It is purely coincidental that our school has the same motto.*

** *Prestbury sewage works is proof that the old adage, "Where there's muck there's money" is true. Home to Manchester United players, this prestigious Cheshire village is jam packed with numerous millionaires. The streets are paved in gold, not because the place offers opportunity to those seeking to make their fortune, but because we just can't help showing the rest of you just how well off we are!*

THE WAR AGAINST OBSCENITY

Concerned by the rise in naughty language, especially amongst young people, the Home Office decided in 2011 to set up a Select Committee chaired by Sir Hugh Swearing MP. Sir Swearing said that proper research was needed to discover the reasons behind the alarming rise in the use of obscenity. As a result a panel of experts was formed consisting of a number of psychologists, sociologists and clairvoyants. This was a panel, said Sir Swearing, which you could swear to. And so he did – frequently. The panel took only 10 minutes to discover the reason *why* young people swear. It was, they said, due to the frequent use of swear words in popular literature. As a result the government set up an Obscene Regulator who would work with the publishing industry and force them to clean up their act. The job of the Regulator is to ensure that publishers replace naughty words with harmless alternatives. Consequently, this book has been checked by the Regulator and any swear words have been replaced. As a result of this prompt action by the government, books for young people are now less harmful and it was all due to Sir Swearing. We can all swear to that.

Carol Singer.

Obscene Regulator.

London 2012.

RE: THE WAR AGAINST OBSCENITY

Blooming hell! The blooming, bloomers, blooming bloomed! Scallywag! Posterior! Poo! Wee-wee! Just checking to see if she's on the ball.

The Author.

Part 1: Introduction
Your Headmaster

Hi, there! I'm Alfred Scholar NUT TA and I live in a palatial mansion in Prestbury, Cheshire. This is where footballers like Wayne Rooney live. Does he still live there? God knows. I wouldn't know because I don't associate myself with common people. Never have done and never will. Rooney probably thinks – or thought if he's moved – that his house was big. *Balderdash!* My mansion is considerably larger than Wayne Rooney's house! Rooney's *house?* Please don't make me laugh. My blooming garden shed's bigger than that. In fact, Rooney's place might just be big enough for my garden gnomes. They can go in there to keep out of the rain. Yes, these are *real* gnomes. I pay them to wear funny outfits and stand around in my garden. Cruel? Ask them. They get paid well for their work. And standing there holding gardening implements and lanterns can hardly be called work. Some even get to sit on the large mushrooms carved out of marble.

From this you'll gather that the head teacher of an independent school must be raking it in. But be warned! Before you all go rushing off to be one, I must point out that not *all* head teachers of independent schools are as well paid as I am. In fact none of them are. And, as for those scallywags in state schools...I carry more loose change in my pockets than they earn in a year! In fact, I get better money than any of my colleagues. And when you read our blog you'll know why. They say money isn't everything. *Rubbish!* Where would you be without money, eh? You'd be living rough on the street selling *The Big Issue.* Well, don't thrust one in my face or you'll get a swift kick up the posterior! The sound of cash is the only thing I listen to. And I'm not talking about the late Johnny Cash, either!

OFSTED!

Even teachers with nerves of steel shiver in fear when they hear that word! But not me...not Alfie Scholar. Oh, no! My nerves are made of titanium. Which is much lighter and stronger than steel. But for those less fortunate than I, cases of chronic and seemingly intractable constipation have been miraculously cured at the very mention of an *OFSTED* inspection. We're talking soiled underwear. We're talking brown stains on the seat of your trousers. The Office for Standards in Education would have everyone believe their job is to ensure each pupil in the UK gets the very best education. But, as my father used to say, you can't bullpoop a bullpooper! And I'll have you know that I'm one of the biggest bullpoopers around. So there! The truth is *OFSTED* was set up by a meddling government with nothing better to do than poke their noses into things that don't concern them. Leave teaching to the teachers, I say! So what exactly what is it *OFSTED* do when they come to inspect a school?

Well, it was King Alfred who coined that famous Anglo-Saxon expression, "They want to know the ins and outs of a cat's anal passage." Only he was applying it to the Vikings who kept asking him how much gold he had. He tried to tell them that money wasn't everything. "Nonsense!" cried the Vikings. "It might not be everything to you, but it is to us!" And, according to our Head of History, that actually happened. Back whenever and wherever it was. And to prove that this story of King Alfred came straight from the lips of the head of our history department I saw them move as he was talking to me. However, I was going over the accounts at the time and I may not have caught *all* his words.

Anyway, that's quite enough about him! This is *my* book. Before moving on to our magnificent blog you'll need to get some idea of what sort of school Wallygrange is. I could have given you extracts from our school prospectus, but our solicitors have advised against it. At least until the court case has been resolved. So, instead, our 6th Form suggested we let you read the *2011 OFSTED* report. The one that totally slagged us off. I won't pull any punches. At Wallygrange we believe in transparency. This is why we wear cellophane clothing. Only joking. We don't wear it all the time. So I must warn you here and now that this report makes grim reading. But you must bear in mind that the report gives only *one* side of the story. *Their* side. I'm not suggesting for one moment *OFSTED* are biased. What I am suggesting is that they sent a young woman to do a man's job. Never a good idea. This was the first school she'd ever inspected. And she did so with no support from her colleagues. In those circumstances how on earth could she be expected to do a good job? Obviously, we ourselves couldn't give her any support. After all, it's not our job to help these people. So my advice to the reader is to look at this report objectively and ignore any negative aspects because these will inevitably prejudice your opinion.

In this extract of the report you'll get a picture of our school and the people that inhabit it. Some may call them weird. Okay, we live in a democracy and they're entitled to their opinions. However, in my view these opinions are prejudicial and highly flammable. So flammable it's a miracle the people who hold them don't burst into flames! Who cares if some of the people here at Wallygrange are weird? They certainly don't. They get paid the same as everyone else. Anyway, I wrote this book because I wanted to put the record straight. And I'd like to finish with these words. *OFSTED* said we were the worst. Well, they've had their say and now I'm having mine. And I'll leave the good people of Prestbury and the rest of the world to decide if *OFSTED* were right.

Actually I haven't *quite* finished with this rant. That's because the *OFSTED* report continues to stick in my craw. And will remain there until I finally shuffle off this mortal coil. You will see that one of the accusations levelled in the *OFSTED* report was that I employed teachers *not* for their teaching abilities, but because they couldn't get a job in any other school. That I searched high and low for the most incompetent teachers in the country. And that I even paid some of them to *be* incompetent! And that none of the teachers, including myself, had any genuine qualifications at all! In my defence I can only point out that paper qualifications aren't everything and that many of my staff gained their knowledge at the school of hard knocks, (in the case of our senior caretaker, a former SAS man, some of those knocks were very hard indeed).

Below you'll find the totally biased and one sided *OFSTED* report which attempted to cast aspersions on the finest grammar school in *this* land or any other - and that's no idle boast.

The inspection was conducted by Elizabeth Merryweather who, I can say without any fear of contradiction, was totally unsuited for the job. She was not, to use a popular buzz word, fit for purpose and quite clearly well out of her depth. But don't just take *my* word for it. No! Read the report. Read it with an open mind. Read it objectively. Try to forget that I'm regarded by my staff and pupils as the greatest headmaster of all time. As for transparency? Ask any of them and they'll tell you they can see right through me! Then make up your own minds…

The Totally Biased and One Sided Report of the Wallygrange Grammar School Inspection, 2011

"I must first apologise for the delay in making my report. I've just finished my counselling sessions and the doctor says I'm ready to put my experiences down on paper. He says it will help me come to terms with what has happened to me. I was warned about Wallygrange. When they heard I'd been assigned to inspect the place my colleagues told me not to come within a million miles of the school. They advised me to report sick. They spoke of gross incompetence on the part of the teaching staff. They told me there was no discipline. They said the headmaster was a compulsive liar who couldn't tell the truth to save his own life. They spoke of fraud. Of happenings so strange they made crop circles and UFO abductions look commonplace. They said the place was haunted. That it was being used by the government to conduct weird experiments. That it had been taken over by aliens. And when they told me that the other members of the inspection team were off sick and that I'd have to do it on my own, I should have refused. But I was new in the job and this would be my first inspection so I was determined to show them I could do it. So, like a fool, I decided to go there with an open mind. I was sure they were exaggerating. After all, no school could be that bad. In the event I was wrong and they were right. I barely managed to escape from that hellhole with my life. Even worse, I had to leave part of my body behind. My union have told me to start legal proceedings to get compensation, but I'm not hopeful. After all, who's going to believe I was scalped by Big Chief Sitting Bull?

I'd set out early and arrived in Prestbury at 8.43 am as the pupils were arriving. There was something about them I couldn't quite fathom. A haunted look on their faces. It was the look of an animal in a laboratory cage. An animal that senses there's something not quite right about the place, but just can't figure out what it is. My first shock came when I pulled into the staff parking space. No sooner had I stopped than this man in his early-thirties came running out of the main building and knelt down by the side of my car. His shifty little eyes reminded me of a confidence trickster, but I told myself you can't tell a book by its cover. How wrong I was! At first I felt sorry for him. Seeing tears streaming down his face I thought there must have been some ghastly accident. As I got out he introduced himself as the Headmaster, Alfred Scholar NUT TA. 'Please don't be too hard on me!' he begged. 'I need this job to support my wife and our four-hundred children!'

For a moment I thought I'd misheard him. 'Four hundred?' I asked.

He corrected himself. 'Four hundred and three. She gave birth to some triplets last night!' I was about to remark that his poor wife must be exhausted when he asked me if I was married and had any children. I said yes. He said in that case I'd know how expensive it was bringing them up. I told him I only had two, not four hundred and three. He then asked me to imagine having to buy top-of-the-range designer label trainers for them all. Not just ordinary trainers, either. But those with the flashing lights on the soles. He said at night his house was lit up like the Blackpool Illuminations. And then there was the fact that they all supported

Manchester United. Did I have any idea how much four hundred and three home and away kits cost him?

Telling him that I didn't believe a word he was saying only produced a fresh torrent of tears. Worse still, the buffoon actually began kissing my shoes! Yes, I'm sorry! I realise calling people names is a highly unprofessional way for an OFSTED Inspector to behave. But I can't help it. I've never been so disgusted in my life. When I asked him if he was a man or a mouse, he pulled a large wedge of cheese from his pocket and began nibbling at it. I ordered him to get a grip on himself and show me to his office. Then came my second shock. As we walked to the door a foul smell hit me. It was like raw sewage. I looked at the Headmaster who was still nibbling on his wedge of Cheddar. Had he just passed wind? I told him if that's what cheese does to him he should see a doctor. He merely sniggered. I knew then that this would be no ordinary school.

I was right. The proof came when we walked down the corridor. As we turned a corner I noticed some suspicious looking teenagers standing around a large soft drinks dispensing machine. They had hoods pulled over their faces and one was holding a screwdriver. To me it looked like he was trying to lever the panel off so he could get at the money inside. Seeing I was watching them, the youths began to make rude gestures. But when I pointed this out to Scholar he seemed unperturbed.

'Oh, don't worry about them,' he said. 'They're doing community service and helping one of the assistant school caretakers, Joseph Starlin.'

'Joseph Starlin?'

Scholar looked at me. 'Yes, do you know him?'

I shook my head. 'No, it's just that the name rang a bell.'

'So it should, love,' said Scholar. 'Ringing the bell is one of his jobs.'

I had to explain to him that that wasn't what I'd meant. I merely meant that the assistant school caretaker had the same name as the infamous communist dictator. At which point Scholar looked puzzled and asked, 'What communist dictator?'

I expressed my surprise that Scholar, a teacher, had never heard of Joseph Stalin. 'It's clear, Mr Scholar,' I said, 'That history is not your subject.' He ignored the sarcasm and delivered a tirade against the stupidity of learning a lot of useless facts about the past. 'Who the hell,' he asked me, 'wants to know about the pyramids or the Great Freeze of London, eh?'

'Surely you mean the Great Fire of London.'

'Whatever," Scholar replied with a shrug of his shoulders. He then indicated that we'd reached his office. By now I'd gained the distinct impression that Scholar's level of intelligence was much lower than that of most living creatures. Probably at the level of those single-celled organisms that live in ponds. Let me put it this way: if brains were dynamite this idiot didn't have enough to blow his cap off. Yet as we entered his office I saw that the walls were plastered with diplomas and university degrees. Scholar could see I was impressed. He pointed to two of them. One said he was a fully qualified brain surgeon and the other was the Nobel Prize in Arithmetic!

I asked him how many brains he'd operated on. 'I've lost count,' he said dismissively. It's just a hobby of mine.' He then pointed to the diploma next to it.

'Not bad, eh?' said Scholar smugly. 'The Nobel Prize in Arithmetic for someone who can't even recite the seven times table.'

My head was beginning to swim. 'I beg your pardon?' I said.

Scholar explained that he could recite most of the others without having to count on his fingers. But that there was something about the number seven that just baffled him. I told him that there was just one slight problem with that award. There's no such thing as a Nobel Prize in Mathematics, *let alone Arithmetic!*

'Are you saying I'm a fraud?' cried Scholar. I could tell he was getting hot under the collar because his shirt caught fire. So we stood there for a while trading insults. He gave me one of his for two of mine. Finally I remembered who I was and apologised for my unprofessional behaviour. Scholar said he'd forgive me if I gave him and his school a glowing report. I told him I couldn't do that. 'Ah, well, it was worth a try,' he said, shrugging his shoulders.

The display on the walls intrigued me. It was part of my job to make an assessment of the head teacher and there seemed to be no limit to this man's accomplishments. So I pointed to another certificate – this one purported to be from NASA stating that he'd walked on the moon with Buzz Aldrin. It came with an obviously faked photograph of Scholar standing next to Aldrin as they posed by the lunar module.

At this Scholar looked annoyed. 'Okay, Mrs Clever-Clogs,' he cried. 'Just what makes you think it's a fake?'

'Buzz Aldrin is wearing a spacesuit,' I said, 'but you're not. In which case you'd have been dead as soon as you opened the hatch and climbed outside. Unless,' I added sarcastically, 'your brilliant mind worked out a way of extracting oxygen from a vacuum.'

There was a pause and then Scholar grinned. 'I wanted to hire a spacesuit," he confessed. 'But it was too expensive. Actually, most pupils and their parents think it's the real thing. In fact, 'the Sixth Form produced created it for me.' He paused to wipe some crumbs from his mouth. 'They can do you one if you want. It'll impress your bosses no end. First woman on the moon? How's that for gender equality? All Pankhurst did was chain herself to some railings. But by stepping on the lunar surface you'll have achieved far more than she ever did.'

I told him I had to decline his kind offer to help me enhance the cause of women's liberation. I then asked him if any of them were genuine

'Oh yes,' he said. 'They're all registered with the school.'

I told him I meant the awards on the wall, not the Sixth Formers. He just shrugged as he plonked himself down behind his desk. 'I think a couple might be,' he said. 'But I can't remember which ones.' I pulled myself together. Something about this place was having an adverse affect on me and I had a sudden vision of ending up a gibbering idiot like the Headmaster. Maybe there was some kind of pollution in the air. Maybe that smell hadn't come from Scholar's nether regions...

'Are you all right?' asked Scholar. 'You look a little pale.'

'I'm fine,' I said, sitting down and taking my notebook from my attaché case. First I asked him how long he'd been the Headmaster at Wallygrange. 'About ten years now,' he said. I watched in amazement as he began taking his shoes and socks off. 'I took over from my late father, who was the previous headmaster. He was found in the science block dead as a doornail with his head in a bucket of sulphuric acid.' At this point Scholar grunted as he lifted one leg and put his foot on the desk. Then, taking out a pair of industrial sized nail clippers, he began cutting his toenails. I ducked as one particularly large one missed me by about an inch and ricochet off the wall.

'I wouldn't sit too close,' he said. 'Last time my secretary nearly choked on one. She was yawning at the time and the clipping from my big toe went down her throat.' I moved my chair back.

'What did the coroner say?' I asked.

Scholar looked puzzled. 'You don't call the coroner just because someone swallows a toenail,' he said. 'Not unless they've choked on the scallywag.'

'I was talking about your poor father who was found with his head in a bucket of sulphuric acid.'

'Ah!' cried Scholar. 'Actually, his head wasn't in the bucket. Well, it had been. But by the time they found him it had all but dissolved...apart from his left eye, that is. It was lying on the bottom staring up at them.'

'His left eye?' I croaked.

Scholar scratched his head. 'Come to think of it, it could have been his right one. They both looked the same. Anyway, he'd also been severely beaten with a mop, had a carving knife in his back and his limbs had been chopped off with a chainsaw. The police suspected foul play and later arrested one of the science teachers, along with the caretaker, the cook, the cleaner...and pretty much anyone else they could lay their hands on.'

I told him that these were clearly not normal run-of-the-mill problems.

'Correct,' said Scholar, 'but remember that Wallygrange is not your normal run-of-the-mill school. Because of this unfortunate incident, a number of parents wanted to remove their children. Fortunately the teaching staff refused to let them. Later, when the Head of PE exploded after drinking too much of that muscle building concoction they sell in health food shops, morale at the school sank to a new low. As a result of this, the School Governors decided that some new blood was needed. A few days later, the Head of Respect provided lots of it when he severed an artery whilst carving some graffiti in the staff washroom using a Stanley knife.'

I paused to take this in. 'I see. And just what sort of graffiti was he carving?'

'It was a naughty word.'

The incident, if true, intrigued me. I'd never heard of a teacher carving naughty words in a washroom. On the other hand, it could have been another of Scholar's ridiculous stories. The medical profession have a term for it. The Munchausen Syndrome. It refers to a person who lives in a world of fantasy. A description that seemed to fit Scholar perfectly. 'What naughty word?' I asked.

Scholar looked worried. 'If I tell you, you might order me to wash my mouth out with soap.'

'I won't do that.'

'Oh,' said Scholar, sounding disappointed. 'I was hoping you might. Anyway, the naughty word was "Poulet."'

'That's not naughty,' I said. 'That's French for "chicken."'

'It is?' said Scholar. 'Well, fancy that. Anyway, it was at this point that I was appointed.'

'Yes, I heard about that,' I said. 'According to my information, the school governors only interviewed one applicant for the post...and that was you. Don't you think that was a little irregular?'

Scholar seemed unperturbed. 'I know what you're implying, but it was all proper and above board. The Chairman of the Board of Governors read through the various CV's that were submitted and considered there was really only one person suitable for the job.'

'I see. And who is the Chairman of the Board of Governors?'

'I am.'

I told him that it didn't need Sherlock Holmes to work out that this all looked highly suspicious. At which point Scholar winked and told me that his choice had clearly been the right one. And why? Because in the space of one week he'd managed to turn the whole school around.

'And how did you do that?' I asked.

'Well,' said Scholar, 'previously, the front entrance had been facing north. But, with some remarkable engineering ingenuity involving several bags of sugar and industrial fertilizer plus some sticks of dynamite, the main entrance is now facing south.'

I struggled to take this information in. Either he was an unmitigated liar or the greatest structural engineer since Isambard Kingdom Brunel! Looking at the fakes hanging on his walls I plumped for the former. On the other hand, from what I'd seen already I reckoned that anything was possible.

'Take a gander at the school rules,' said Scholar. He got up off the chair and walked towards the filing cabinet in the corner. As he did so he let out a resounding fart. Wafting his hand behind his huge posterior to disperse the cabbage like aroma, he turned to me and smiled.

'My mother always says, '"Wherever thou may be, let thy wind go free."'

'Your mother sounds like quite a character,' I said, putting a tissue to my nose.

'She is,' said Scholar. 'You'll probably meet her. She's one of the dinner ladies along with Her Grace the Duchess of Addlington'

I expressed my surprise. 'The Duchess of Addlington?'

'That's right,' said Scholar. 'Your hearing's pretty good. Not like my mother. She's as deaf as a post. And as daft as one. Anyway, Her Grace is a nice old bird. A bit toffee nosed. I have a lick of it now and then.' He paused as if waiting for my reaction. 'That was a joke,' he said.

'Are you sure?' I said sarcastically. After the incident with my shoes the thought of Scholar licking the noses of his staff didn't seem so unusual at all.

'Absolutely!' said Scholar. 'I only lick it as a joke. After she's picked it, of course. Hygiene, you see.'

After reading it I threw the file on the desk in disgust. 'These rules are totally ridiculous!' I cried. 'Not only that, they breach the pupil's basic Human Rights. These rules are set out in such a way as to make it impossible not to break them. How on earth can any pupil be expected to abide by them and avoid paying a fine? You must be raking in a fortune! How much are you making a week from fines?'

'About £12,800.'

'And what happens to this money?'

Scholar shrugged. 'The School Treasurer deals with all that.'

When I reminded Scholar that, apart from all his other jobs, he was the also the School Treasurer he winked. I had to restrain the urge to get up and hit him. 'I really must insist that these rules are rescinded immediately.' He looked puzzled.

'Rescinded?'

'Sorry,' I said. 'I forgot I'm dealing with an illiterate oaf. Rescinded means removed... stopped. They are clearly illegal. We live in a democracy. These rules are more suited for a totalitarian dictatorship. Hitler and Mussolini would have used these rules. They are totally unacceptable in an English school. They'll have to go.'

Scholar shook his head. 'I asked the School Solicitor and he said they were perfectly legal.'

'And who is the...?' I stopped as Scholar pointed to one of the certificates on the wall. 'In other words,' I said, 'you're also the School Solicitor?'

He nodded.

'I suppose,' I asked sarcastically, *'you'll be telling us next you're also the Chief Bottle Washer?'*

He nodded.

By now I was totally exasperated. I asked him how the school dealt with matters of discipline. Scholar proceeded to inform me that he'd introduced a very effective system of detention. He then went on to describe in some detail how the offender's hands and feet are tied together and then they're gagged. Thus secured, a hood is placed over their heads before they're sealed inside an airtight metal container which is then buried 900 metres underground. Scholar explained that the term for this form of detention is Behaviour Modification Using Deep Isolation or BMUDI. *I asked him how many pupils are presently undergoing* BMUDI.

'Let me check,' he said. *He entered something on his computer and smiled. 'At the moment there are only two. Hopefully, we'll remember where we buried them!' Seeing my look of horror he hastily added that that had been a joke. I wish I could have believed him. I made a note to inform the emergency services.*

I then held up OFSTED's *information sheet about his school and pointed to some glaring discrepancies. For example, the Deputy Headmaster's name was Alfred Scholar NUT TA. Was he any relation?*

'Yes, that's me,' said Scholar.

I told him that he couldn't be the Headmaster and *the deputy Headmaster at the same time. Nobody could. It just wasn't physically possible. Scholar looked doubtful so I had to explain that the human body was incapable of being in two places at the same time. Maybe in a few hundred years we might have the technology to do that. But not right now. So, if he was ill or away at a conference who was there to stand in for him? Scholar replied that the senior teacher would take charge. I asked Scholar who the senior teacher was.*

'That's me again,' announced Scholar with a big grin on his face.

'Just let me get this straight,' I said, "Are you saying that when you're not here, the school is left without any form of leadership?"

Scholar laughed. 'Good God, woman!' he cried. 'The teachers at Wallygrange don't need any leadership. They know what they have to do. They have to teach the pupils, that's their job. End of story.'

'If we were to follow that logic,' I told him, 'then there's no need for a Headmaster or a Deputy Headmaster. In other words, you've just talked yourself out of a job.'

Scholar replied that he was here as a precaution. Just in case there was ever any need for a leader. And, anyway, he wasn't about to give up a good paying job like this. There was clearly no arguing with a man like that, so I decided to drop the subject for the time being. I did, however, ask him why he was also the head of the school accounts department. He pointed to one of the diplomas. It was for a degree in Accountancy from the Chopastickee College in Peking.

'It looks as dodgy as those other ones,' I said.

Scholar refused to answer and merely tapped the side of his nose. I then asked him about his relationship with the pupils and their parents. Was he readily available for advice and consultation? Scholar assured me that his office was open for approximately eight seconds a day should pupils or parents wish to drop in for a quick chat.

'Eight seconds?' I said. 'It would have to be quick. So just what do you do for the rest of the day?'

Scholar winked and tapped his nose again. 'That's for me to know and you to find out.'

'Yes, Mr Scholar,' I snapped. *'And that's precisely what I'm going to do.'*

I then turned to the school curriculum. I asked Scholar to describe the range of subjects at Wallygrange. He began by telling me that there were an infinite range of opportunities open to the pupils. I laughed and said surely that was an exaggeration. This angered him.

'Let me give you some idea of just how vast this range, is,' he said. *'Imagine counting every grain of sand on earth and then multiplying that number by eight hundred billion. And that's just the number of abilities open to each pupil on the first day of term!'*

'You mean there's more?' I said.

He nodded. He then went on to claim that after that the number of opportunities quadrupled every second of the day. (Not counting holidays when this number was reduced by fifteen-point-eight percent). Scholar concluded by boasting that by the time the pupil left Wallygrange he or she would possess enough GCSE's to fill the known universe ten times over. He concluded by telling me that not many schools could make that sort of claim! I told him that at least was something we could both agree on. In fact, no other school would dare to make such an outrageous one.

'Damn right!' said Scholar, banging his fist on the desk. *'And why? Because they know they're not in our league.'*

I jokingly remarked I wouldn't be surprised if Scholar didn't have a framed certificate on his wall declaring that his school produced the world's most educated pupils. Whereupon Scholar told me that the Sixth Form were in the process of designing one. I was determined to show this man up for a liar, so I asked to see a list of the infinite number of subjects taught in his remarkable school. I added that I doubted there was enough paper to print it on, even if one recycled every scrap and stripped every forest on earth! By now I should have realised that Scholar had an answer for everything. He explained that the number of subjects taught at Wallygrange depended, not only on the size of the teaching staff, but also on their goodwill and cooperation.

'Teachers are only human,' he said. After thinking about it for a moment he added, *'Well, most of them are.'*

I asked him what he meant by that and he told that at least one of them had been cloned by the 6th Form. There may have been others, but he couldn't be quite sure. Then he told me that there were times when the teachers preferred to stay in bed rather than come to school. Especially in winter when it was cold outside. Then there was the question of memory. Teachers sometimes forgot things. For example, they might sometimes forget what subject they're supposed to teach. This might be due to old age. Apparently some of Scholar's staff are over a hundred years old!

'Anything else?' I asked.

Scholar nodded and told me that the Gooseberry Wine often had a disastrous effect on the memory. When I looked puzzled he took a bottle out of his desk drawer and held it up. "One of our Sixth Formers, a lad called Wheek, makes a wine out of gooseberries. He's brilliant at it, but then he should be. His father is a local brewer. Have you ever tried Wheek Beer?"

I told him I was a teetotaller.

'A golf fanatic, eh?' said Scholar.

I asked him what he was blabbering on about. *'I meant,'* Scholar explained. *'That you're one of those people who count the tees on a golf course. A teetotaller.'*

He sounded perfectly serious, so I assumed he actually thought there were people who went around golf courses counting tees. I told him that the term normally applied to people who didn't touch alcohol.

'Ah,' said Scholar. 'One of them, are you? Well, Wheek Beer is nice but it's not as potent as this Gooseberry Wine.'

'I'll take your word for it," I remarked, adding that the Sixth Form seemed to have a number of extra-curricular activities. Scholar took a swig from the bottle and belched. 'They have a finger in everything,' he said. 'I've told them it's unhygienic, but you know what teenagers are like. They just won't listen to us old flatulents.' He held the bottle out to me. 'Are you sure you don't want some? This stuff will help you see things in a different way.'

I shook my head.

Scholar shrugged and took another swig. In which case, he said, the relevant lessons had to be cancelled. On top of this, in order to teach all these subjects they also needed enough teachers to fill the known universe ten times over. And they were having trouble with that one.

I had another stab at sarcasm. 'Ask your wife,' I said. 'Perhaps she could give birth to them.' Scholar ignored this and continued swigging from the bottle. He explained that if a teacher did forget then the pupils were requested to remain at their desks until such time the teacher regained his/her memory. Failing that, until the bell rang. I said sarcastically. 'You certainly have a novel way of educating your pupils.' But there was no response from Scholar who was just sitting there with a blank expression on his face. Then I noticed that he'd finished the bottle. 'Are you all right, Mr Scholar?' I asked.

'Where am I?' he said. 'What's more to the point...who am I?'

I told him that Wheek should forget the gooseberries and use Forget-Me-Nots instead.

Signed: Elizabeth Merryweather."

After reading the *OFSTED* report you've no doubt decided that the poor woman was clearly deranged. And I don't blame you. Good for you! The same thought went through *my* head when I read it. That and several others. But, unlike you, I'm a headmaster and I don't go by my feelings alone. Even when those feelings threaten to engulf me. So I asked myself some technical questions. Questions we teachers ask when faced with negative assessments of our professional standards. Questions like: don't *OFSTED* have a system whereby they assess the mental state of their inspectors? Or do they have a recruitment policy that states they must give preference to candidates with severe mental health issues? Debilitating mental health issues. Yes, I know we should be doing our bit to reintegrate these poor people into the community. But how can giving them a job with *OFSTED* help? Do they imagine that inspecting schools is therapeutic? But that's my problem, not yours.

So, here's our blog. And, after you've read it, I know you'll feel that you must offer our school your full support. In fact, this will become your sole reason for living. And that's no exaggeration. As a result you'll see no other alternative but to make a generous donation to the Wallygrange Headmaster's Aid Fund. And to keep making one, come what may. No sacrifice will be too great. In fact, there are times when I've almost donated to it myself! This would be like a beggar putting his own money in his begging bowl! The extracts, which relate to 2012, are not dated because I've chosen only the most interesting ones. Well, let's just say that after taking legal advice these were the only ones safe to print. But first a word from our sponsors...

HINSHAWS SKIP HIRE.

Is your child eating too much fast food and getting little by way of exercise? Then hire a skipping rope from Hinshaws and provide them with hours of fun!

THE CHESHIRE BULBING SOCIETY.

This is a place where gardeners meet to discuss their favourite hobby!

MACK'S MINI TRANSPORT.

Let me transport your goods or possessions in my 1964 Austin Mini, (size and weight restrictions may apply).

Part 2:
The Wallygrange Grammar School Blog

Although the original idea came from me the blog that finally emerged was the result of a meeting I had with our School Captain, Tom Brown. To give readers a flavour of the intense and sometimes heated discussion that took place I've included an excerpt from a transcript of our conversation. Yes, my office is bugged! As is the rest of the school. But the decision to include audio recordings as well as CCTV in every nook and cranny at Wallygrange School was one that I did not take lightly. I'm not by nature a snooper and the rumours that I was a Peeping Tom in my youth are entirely unfounded. I was a bird watcher. Like Bill Oddie. It's as simple as that. And yes, regardless of what my detractors may say, you *can* find our feathered friends in cities and towns in the dead of night. Even in public toilets. Some birds are nocturnal. The owl, for one. It's true that most owls refuse to nest in people's bedrooms. But there's always that frisson of excitement at finding that one owl who has decided to go for an alternative lifestyle. As for the hidden microphones here at the school? So what? Even the high and mighty have bugged their workplaces. Richard Nixon is just one example.

But I don't know why I'm trying to justify my actions. Why should I? I'm the Headmaster and I can do as I damn well please. So here's the transcript...

Transcript of Conversation: Thursday, September 15th. Headmaster's Study, Wallygrange Grammar School. Present: Alfred Scholar NUT TA, Tom Brown, School Captain.

TB: *We can open the blog to all and sundry.*

Alfred Scholar NUT TA: *Fair enough. I don't mind two extra people reading it.*

TB: *I don't get you. What two extra people?*

Alfred Scholar NUT TA: *All and Sundry. The last one sounds Indian.*

TB: You're serious, right?

Alfred Scholar NUT TA: *Of course I'm serious. There's a time for joking and a time to be serious. This is a time to be serious.*

TB: *You're actually telling me you don't know what "all and sundry" means?*

Alfred Scholar NUT TA: *I'm not that stupid. Or am I? That's for me to know and you to find out. And good luck to you!*

(Tom Brown starts laughing).

Alfred Scholar NUT TA: *Have some more Gooseberry Wine.*

TB: *No thank you, sir. As I said, by making the blog available to a wider audience we can show* OFSTED *that we're not hiding anything. That by hanging our dirty washing out people will see that we've got nothing to hide.'*

Alfred Scholar NUT TA: *No problemo. I'm no stranger to that. My wife always hung our dirty washing out. Until she learned how to use the washing machine.*

TB: *I didn't mean* that *sort of washing. It was a metaphor. You do know what a metaphor is?*

Alfred Scholar NUT TA: *Yes. From the sound of it, it can't be cleaned and has to be hung out dirty.*

TB: *Please don't take this the wrong way, sir. But most of the pupils think you're a very disturbed person.*

Alfred Scholar NUT TA: *Do they indeed?*

TB: *Yes, and I think you should just listen. So I'll explain it once more. By restricting access to the blog people might think you're frightened of something. Now it could be a gamble, given the negative things that have been said about us. But, given your regular visits to Las Vegas and Monte Carlo, I get a feeling you like to gamble.*

Alfred Scholar NUT TA: *You bet I do! In fact, I'll bet you a hundred quid that I do. Are you on?*

TB: *I think I'll pass on that one.*

Alfred Scholar NUT TA: Pah! *What a wimp. Scared of losing your money? I'm not.*

TB: *But, sir. It's not* your *money you lose...it's the school's.*

Alfred Scholar NUT TA: *I am the school! You need to spread your wings. At your age I was at the greyhound track nobbling the dogs.*

TB: *Nobbling the dogs?*

Alfred Scholar NUT TA: *Give the favourite a few steak pies...that soon slows them down. Don't get me wrong. The wife and I love dogs. We love them to distraction. Others would have doped them with chemicals. Not me. From me they got Holland's Pies. Okay, Brown! To hell with it! We'll go viral with the bog.*

TB: *Warts and all? There could be some big warts.*

Alfred Scholar NUT TA: *So what? Old Cromwell had them.*

TB: *Yes, I know Cromwell had warts. But what the devil has that got to do with it?*

Alfred Scholar NUT TA: *Even with warts he chopped the bishop's head off!*

TB: *It was the king. And he didn't chop it off - he got the Executioner to do it.*

Alfred Scholar NUT TA: *Whatever! The point is I'm the headmaster and we'll do the blog my way!*

TB: *And what way is that?'*

Alfred Scholar NUT TA: *The way you suggested we do it.*

So the blog was set up and below was the very first post...

IF THEY THINK OUR DAYS ARE NUMBERED, THEY CAN THINK AGAIN!

OFSTED and the Department of Education want to close us down! How dare they? They don't give a damn about the children – they just want to get back at me. This is how ungrateful they are. I offered them a perfectly reasonable backhander and they turned it down. Can you believe that? I can't. It's clear these people have never worked in industry where backhanders are a way of life. Maybe they thought they were making quite enough money out of the poor taxpayers! In fact, if I was a taxpayer I'd be very angry indeed. All that money spent on hounding poor teachers who have enough on their plates without that lot breathing down their necks. Fortunately I have a very good accountant who's shown me how to avoid paying taxes. So, let's all support this blog and show *OFSTED* they can't dictate to us Wallygrangers! Let's show them we're made of stronger stuff.

Posted by Alfred Scholar NUT TA

I followed this up with a hard hitting explanation of just what I hoped to achieve with the blog...

WHO IS THE BLOG FOR?

This blog was initially intended for the staff of Wallygrange Grammar School and I wasn't going to include the pupils or their parents. Why? Because I'd heard that other schools had appeared on social network sites and had negative comments from ungrateful brats who thought they could insult their teachers! Well, let me tell you here and now that things don't work that way at Wallygrange. Here it's the other way round. Here at Wallygrange the only people who are allowed to hurl insults about are teachers. That's what they've been trained to do. However, Tom Brown, our School Captain, suggested that I allow the whole world to see our blog. At first I was sceptical. I'm no one's glove puppet and I wasn't about to have someone shove their hand up my fundamental orifice and control my body. Especially not the hand of some spotty 17 year old! But he said it was an excellent way to show *OFSTED,* and the world at large, that we weren't as incompetent as the report made out. As soon as I heard those dulcet tones was hooked! Ah, the exuberance and sheer wisdom of youth! I was once just like Tom. I don't exactly know when that was, but I'm almost sure it happened at some point or another. My other stipulation

----

At this point I suffered from what we authors call, "writer's block." There was only thing I could do and that was to recklessly indulge myself in my favourite libation and pray the muse would return to me. So finally, after a refreshing glass of Gooseberry Wine I was back in full fettle...

WHO IS THE BLOG FOR? (PART 2)

There's nothing like Wheek's remarkable Gooseberry Wine. Literally, as those who've imbibed it will tell you, it gives you a truly mind bending experience. Or should that be mind breaking? Its healing power has enabled me to finish what I'd intended to say in my last post. When constructing this blog I made just one stipulation: that the blog site we use is a free one. I'll be perfectly frank about this: I'd rather see the funds allocated to this project end up *my* pocket than in the pocket of some computer geek.

Having picked the blog the next step was to decide what sort of stuff to put in it. I'm not boasting when I tell you that the intellectual challenge this little conundrum raised gave me quite a buzz. I live by my wits and I love pitting my grey matter against problems like this. What to put in it? I wrestled with that problem all night. Tossing and turning like a headbanger high on Ecstasy as I went through all the options. And, when the dawn's cold light finally fell upon me, I was exhausted and soaked in sweat. But I had the answer! It's a school blog so it should contain things about the school.

But it won't *all* be serious. So for some light relief I'll be indulging in the usual malicious tittle-tattle about pupils, parents and staff. The old way is out. Paperless offices, that's what we want! Give the trees a rest. Let's go green and repair the ozone layer! In short we must move with the times and embrace this new technology lest we become extinct through global warming. Like that pet the Flintstones had. What was it? A Dino-something. We don't want future generations to say the human race was crushed under the weight of their enormous carbon footprints. Or suffocated in their sleep by their smelly greenhouse gasses. What a horrible end to a species like us. That would never do.

And here's some good news...some *paperless* good news! Following the malfunction of one of our nuclear powered toilets, I'm happy to announce that young Charley Muffin from Year 4 has almost totally recovered. According to his mother there are just a few bits of his body that continue to glow in the dark. However, she's asked me to spare her son's blushes by not mentioning what those bits are. And, as long as she doesn't cancel her Direct Debit at the bank, I'll keep my side of the bargain. Fair enough? I thought so.

Posted by Alfred Scholar NUT TA

All right, the initial reaction had been somewhat muted. I think in the first fortnight we had, roughly speaking about three or four visitors. However, the evidence suggested - to me at least – that it was more or less certain our blog would go viral. Not only that, but it would go viral in a really *big way. So I felt I had to introduce myself. Pupils and staff who have seen me know what I look like. But the blog would also be available to strangers. And I wanted to be more that just someone's fingers on a keyboard. I wanted to put some flesh on those fingers...*

TO THOSE VISITING THE WALLYGRANGE GRAMMAR SCHOOL BLOG!

My name is Alfred Scholar NUT TA, and I'm the Headmaster of Wallygrange Grammar School. The school *OFSTED* branded as the "worst in the UK, if not in the entire world!" A ringing endorsement indeed. Except that it rings the wrong note. Legal restraints mean that there's not that much I can – or will – say about myself. Except that I was born a baby and obtained my many distinguished academic qualifications from internet mail order firms. And who hasn't these days? The World Wide Web can turn even those as thick as two short planks into intellectuals. And why not? Equal IQ's for all, that's what I say. My detractors, and there are a few, claim that the pupils of WGS are here merely to fill the Headmaster's bank account. *Wrong!* It's their parents that keep the school running. The money raised from the pupils by fines represents a paltry amount. Hardly enough to pay for the champagne the wife and I get through each week. Yes, I do take some of the money we raise to pay myself a bonus. If the bankers can get away with it then so can I. What's good for the goose, right? In this case the *Golden* Goose.

How much of a bonus do I pay myself? Well, that's for my bank manager to know and others to find out. If they can.

Posted by Alfred Scholar NUT TA

"Mission statements!" Now there's another great buzz word. Wallygrange definitely needed one of those...

THE WALLYGRANGE MISSION STATEMENT

Here at Wallygrange Grammar School we believe in leading. For example, if we find a pupil is trying to pull a fast one, we'll lead him up the garden path. If a pupil's behaviour is good we'll lead them astray. And, if we find that any of our pupils have a musical gift, then we'll lead them a merry dance.

Posted by Alfred Scholar NUT TA

RAISING FUNDS FOR THE SCHOOL

One popular source of income is money laundering. Let's face it, there's nothing worse than taking a £10 or £20 note from the cash dispenser only to find it's grubby, (the note I mean, not the cash dispenser.) Not to mention all the dirty coins circulating around. Think of the germs. It's a wonder most of us haven't come down with MRSC, or whatever. So the 6th Form have developed a machine that washes dirty money. Coins come out sparkling clean and notes are ironed out on a steam press. So, for a nominal fee of 95% + VAT, your money will be so clean you can eat your dinner on it. If there's enough left to buy dinner, that is!

Posted by Alfred Scholar NUT TA

Discipline is a vital ingredient in any school. I think of it as the self-raising flour that makes the establishment rise. Is that the right word to use? Perhaps I've been watching too many episodes of "The Great British Bake Off." Who cares? I don't, that's for sure. What I do know is that children need rules. Not the ones they use to measure things. But the ones that provide a sound structure that will restrain a child's natural instincts to rebel. Forget your complex child psychology with its Formative Years. Forget Freud and his theory that children enjoy defecating and like to play with their faeces. Yes, it's true. And even I still do it from time to time - although I no longer smear the walls with it. But Freud was trying to be too clever because we all know there's a bit more to growing up than defecation. So forget all that. All a good teacher needs to remember is that children need restraining. Yes, it is that simple. It really is. And, because it's illegal to use physical restraints, you have to use rules. End of story, as they say. The rules at Wallygrange can best be described as being unusually complex. But there's a good reason for that. The complexity keeps the pupils on their toes and makes them think. The staff too, for some of the rules also apply to them. They don't apply to me because you don't hold a whip and thrash yourself. Well, at least not in public. What a person gets up to in their bedroom is between them, whoever or whatever's in there with them and the wallpaper. That's how I look at it.

CHANGES TO THE SCHOOL RULES!

Will all pupils please be advised that the School Rules have, once again, been changed. Yes, I know it's a bind. But those are the rules. The rules make it quite clear that they'll be changed and changed frequently or not as frequently as before depending on my mood at the time. Or perhaps it won't depend on *my* mood but someone else's. It might be *your* mood. So *you* might be to blame for the change in rules. Only I will know for sure. At least some of the time I will. Indeed, this rule itself may or may not be in force at the time you're reading this. It's quite simple to understand if you just stop to think about it. The new School Rules are listed below and will be in force - or not in force - until they're changed again.

Rule 1: Pupils are reminded to stay alert at all times. This is because the school rules are flexible and liable to be changed several times during the day. The Headmaster and his staff are also authorised to make up whatever rules they see fit and are under no obligation to make these rules known to the pupils.

Rule 1(b): This states that Rule 1 may, or may not be, in operation when the pupil arrives at school.

Rule 2: Pupils may be punished for breaking the School Rules or for not breaking them or for both. We would like to remind you that this will depend entirely on the whim of the Headmaster or any member of staff implementing this rule, (this includes the caretaker and his staff, cleaners and kitchen staff. And, yes, it also includes the Lollypop Lady outside and Mr Whoopee who parks his ice cream van outside the school gates in summer).

Rule 3: Care of personal property. All personal property must be clearly marked as follows:

"PROPERTY OF MR ALFRED SCHOLAR NUT TA"

This is especially important in the case of valuable items like jewellery and money. This can be done by attaching a simple luggage label to the jewellery. As for paper currency, simply write the words prominently on the reverse side. Small letters, please. We don't want to deface Her Majestic Majesty's banknotes! Property not marked will be confiscated. Marking items in this way makes it easier to locate the owner should the item be lost. The owner being me, that is. And I'm usually in my office or somewhere else. School uniforms do not need to be marked as they are exempt from this rule. After all, unless you're an adult your uniform certainly won't fit the Headmaster.

Rule 4: School Uniform must be worn at all times. However, please bear in mind that, at the discretion of the Headmaster and his staff, the nature of the school uniform may be changed at any time! Pupils found wearing the incorrect uniform will be fined. Or not fined or both!

Rule 5: Disciplinary action will be taken against any pupil or member of staff who has problems understanding these rules. (Apart from me, that is).

Remember: these rules are necessary for the smooth running of the school.

Posted by Alfred Scholar NUT TA

In the old days grammar schools didn't teach boys how to cook. Cooking was for girls and boys who were in the closet. The ones who would secretly don their mother or sister's clothing and rustle up some gastronomic delight whilst their parents weren't home. Like my brother. Until I caught him. I didn't snitch on him. No, he just kept me well fed for years. In fact, he was a better cook than my mother. Especially his soufflés. Surprising really, I'd always thought he was too soft to beat up an egg! And he didn't just beat them, either! He whipped the beggars! But times have changed and here at Wallygrange we have a Food Technology department that caters for those boys who like to slave over a hot stove.

FOR THE ATTENTION OF YEAR 5

Please note that next week's Food Technology lesson will be about deep-frying with lard. And Ms Golly will be demonstrating how you can deep-fry *any* sort of food – including fruit like apples, oranges and bananas. And that Scottish staple, the Mars bar. And she wants no whinging about cholesterol. One more thing: she also wants pupils to stop giggling simply because she has to come through the door sideways. The local builder says he can't widen it any more without threatening the stability of the building.

Posted by Alfred Scholar NUT TA

Occasionally school business takes me abroad...

GENERAL INFORMATION

I'm flying to Las Vegas and I'll be returning to work next Monday. Yes, I know your lives will seem somehow empty without your Headmaster to guide you down life's rocky road. But until I return all I can do is feel your pain. The aching pain of my staff and pupils as they drift rudderless in a school sans their beloved Headmaster. But what else can I do? Tell me that? I didn't *want* to go. Believe you me, I'd love to be by your side 24/7, but there are other pressing issues I have to deal with. So, once more my wife and I are going to Las Vegas, (sometimes humorously called, "Lost Wages"), hoping to raise some extra funds for the School. Just to keep the pot topped up. You know, we sometimes wonder if we could ever contemplate foregoing our lavish lifestyle – one that makes the royal family in Dubai look like spendthrifts. It would certainly mean more money to run the school. It's only a fleeting thought that comes once in a blue moon. But it quite rightly demonstrates that we're not – as some may think – *totally* driven by greed. That we do have a moral compass, even though we don't see the need to use it very often.

Anyway, that's quite enough soul searching for today. For it's time to wipe away these crocodile tears of self-pity and look forward to our arrival in Las Vegas. This is a great place, even though some of the hotels are said to be owned by the Mob. They say America is the land of opportunity and how right they are when even a group of angry people can own a hotel. There's just one thing that's niggling us. Previously when we've been away on one of our jaunts it seems that some of the staff were bunking off after morning assembly. Look, I don't mind the pupils doing it. Their fees are paid whether they're at school or not. But I do expect my teaching staff to set a good example. Is that too much to ask? Where's your loyalty to the school? Are you a dedicated teacher or a lazy, good for nothing who takes time off whenever they feel like it? Because if you *are* a lazy, good for nothing, then Wallygrange doesn't need you. So why not get a job with *OFSTED?* They're always looking for people like you.

OFSTED! You'll have to excuse me but the Red Mist is rising again. My wife says yes, I *was* cruelly maligned by those buffoons. But I mustn't let them get to me. But then she's not a headmaster. She hasn't had to suffer *OFSTED's* slings and arrows. *OFSTED!* A veritable magnet for gross incompetence! A magnet that draws the lame and lazy like flies drawn to a freshly laid cowpat. Inspectors? Don't make me laugh! They couldn't work out the best way to inspect an empty room. No, all they're good at is writing malignant reports without a thought for the mental anguish this may cause the head teacher. All they seem to think about are the pupils! What effect is the school having on the pupils? What about the head teacher? Any fool can see that *their* needs should be paramount. After all, they're the ones *running* the school! But no! Sod the head teacher. They can get post traumatic stress for all *OFSTED* cares!

Mrs Merryweather...*Mrs?* I ask you, what man in his right sense would marry a totally biased harridan like that? It doesn't make any sense. Her face haunts me. Ugly as sin? I *don't* think so! Compared to her sin is a ravishing beauty! Like some festering gangrenous wound filled to the brim with juicy maggots, her report sought to destroy this great school of ours. The school we love and admire above all else. But this blog will put the record straight. It will be a slap in the face to those in the corridors of power at the Department of Education. Heads will roll...and, if there's any justice in this benighted universe, *hers* will be the first on the chopping block!

There! I feel a lot better for that.

Posted by Alfred Scholar NUT TA.

The blog had enabled the School to connect with people all over the world...

HUBBLE, BUBBLE, TOILET TROUBLE!

We recently received an email from our old friend Luigi Minestrone asking for 7 million bars of our laxative chocolate, (the one derived from Wheek Gooseberry Wine). It seems the residents of his country are suffering from an epidemic of chronic constipation and our 6th Form have promised to work overtime to fill the order.

Posted by Alfred Scholar NUT TA

Having nuclear powered toilets can be something of a challenge to our caretakers. With almost no knowledge of nuclear physics and only a basic grounding in simple plumbing, they do a marvellous job. Yes, there are accidents from time to time. Accidents that require a little more technical finesse. When your ballcock is glowing red and about to implode and start a chain reaction you'll need more than just a bucket and mop.

PUPIL SAFETY

After the recent incident involving one of the Year 9 pupils may I remind all pupils that the school toilet facilities are truly unique. Like the electron particle accelerator and the time machine, they were built by the 6th Form. Controlled by a powerful mainframe computer, each toilet cubicle is powered by a small nuclear reactor situated on the roof. The toilets use a patented steam powered vacuum-inertial-gravity system that is perfectly safe as long as the pupil remembers to follow the detailed 457-page instruction manual. As an added precaution – and in line with the safety regulations laid down by the British Nuclear Industry Security Regulations – special decontamination suits are available from the Senior Caretaker at a small fee. Please note that this is payable in advance. However, my dear wife who is also the School Nurse, would like to remind pupils that if they're suffering from acute diarrhoea – as sometimes happens after having a school lunch – then they must not wear a decontamination suit. If they do, they may not be able to get it off in time.

Posted by Alfred Scholar NUT TA

Amongst the huge plethora of professional qualifications hanging on the walls of my office is a Summa Cum Loudly *Degree in General Safety. It was awarded by the prestigious "Nigerian University of The Highest Possible Education." I came across this seat of learning on an e-mail that had been redirected to my "Junk Mail" folder. And quite rightly so because we all know there's a lot of spam mail out there. In fact I'm not too proud to admit that I distribute a lot of it myself. In my case I discovered that Wheek's Gooseberry Wine has an effect similar to Viagra. The difference being that the wine not only produces an erection but increases the length and girth of the member! And what man in his right mind would turn down an opportunity like that? For a price, of course. Hard cash for a hard on! And it's proved to be a money spinner! In the case of the Nigerian university I just happened to have some spare space on the ceiling so I took the opportunity to gain another certificate.*

Operating solely on the internet The University of the Highest Possible Education is a little expensive. However, there were no courses to learn. This is because they were so confident their students would pass the exam with flying colours, they awarded them the degrees as soon as Paypal *sent them the money. Now what other university would do that, eh? Come on! You tell me! The qualification enables me to tackle safety problems of any magnitude... and beyond. With full confidence. Needless to say, I put these skills to good use here at Wallygrange...*

PUPIL SAFETY (2)

In my capacity as the School Road Safety Officer, I've decided that during the autumn and winter, our pupils must wear the special one-piece vulcanised suit I've developed, (with the aid of the 6th Form.) These vulcanised rubber suits are modelled on the chemical warfare suits made for the army and constructed from old tyres taken from tractors and JCB's. They are extremely hard wearing and can be easily cleaned with a garden hose. During autumn and winter the main roads are particularly dangerous due to fog and ice. The vulcanised suit will protect pupils from serious injury. One of our Year 7 pupils tested the suit by walking across the motorway in thick fog. He was struck by 25 vehicles of different shapes and sizes as he was bounced along the road. And, after all that, he only sustained a few minor cuts and bruises! The vulcanised suits branded under the "Rubber-Dubber" designer label cost £250.25 plus VAT. Optional extras include "breathing holes" to allow air to circulate and plug holes in the soles so that sweat can be drained. Easy terms can be arranged.

"KEEP YOUR CHILD SAFE IN A RUBBER-DUBBER!"

Posted by Alfred Scholar NUT TA

Prestbury is a delightful rural village filled to the brim with millionaires of all shapes and sizes. As a result its narrow streets are chock-a-block from dawn till dusk with Bentleys, BMW's and Range Rovers. Drawn by the mystique that surrounds the super rich, visitors from less affluent areas come to gaze in wonder at its main shopping street. Here the pavements are garishly finished in gold leaf and teeming with Burberry clad yuppies eagerly stripping bare the shops filled with designer gear. But it also has its darker side...

INFORMATION URGENTLY REQUIRED!

The police have asked me to deliver this message. Last Thursday, the 7th June at or about 2.16 pm, a woman walking her dog reported seeing a body lying near some empty bottles in the wood close to Wallygrange Grammar School. The body was that of a bearded man in his late 40's. His appearance was described as scruffy and he appeared to have been living rough. The woman was a consultant ornithologist and when she examined the man she found him to be dead. Unable to get a signal on her mobile she dashed to the school where she raised the alarm. When officers arrived at the scene an hour later the body had gone. On examination the bottles were found to have contained Wheek Gooseberry Wine, a popular beverage especially amongst the homeless. If any staff or pupils have any information or saw anything suspicious in the wood would they contact their local police. They urgently require any information that can help lead them to the whereabouts of this body. So now they want to use us as some sort of Crime Scene Investigators! I told them in no uncertain terms that Wallygrange is a school. Granted we have a forensic laboratory...of sorts. But it's far too busy working on things that must, for the moment at least, remain strictly confidential. No, the police will have to learn to find the body on their own.

Posted by Alfred Scholar NUT TA

IMPORTANT DISCLAIMER!

Following a recent project regarding deep frying fruit in lard, the local education committee have contacted me to make it clear that they strongly disapprove of this practice. I told them that this was a private school, the property of the Headmaster, Alfred Scholar NUT TA and it was none of their business how deep we fry fruit or any other substance. They informed me that they were getting in touch with their legal department. 'Why?' I joked. 'Do *they* want to learn how to deep fry as well?'

Posted by Alfred Scholar NUT TA

ADVICE ON HELPING THE POLICE WITH THEIR ENQUIRIES

My advice is simple: don't do it. Come on! Think about it. If the local Plods are incompetent enough to lose a corpse, why should *we* do their work for them? Let me tell you how incompetent they are. Last year they arrested me for smoking grass. The Magistrates threw it out telling the Plod that if someone wants to mow the lawn and then smoke the cuttings they can do so and good luck to them!

Posted by Alfred Scholar NUT TA

My wife is, amongst many things, a qualified paramedic/masseuse, (the qualification was a "buy one and get one free"). So I had no hesitation in appointing her the School Nurse. As a result she's often consulted on medical matters...

RECENT PUBIC INFESTATION

A number of pupils have asked me this question so I just want to make it clear. These crabs are *not* like the ones you find at the seaside. They live only in the place between your legs. And you can't eat them. We've tried. They're too small. You'd need millions to make a decent meal.

Posted by Doris Scholar. School Nurse.

A good head teacher will often bend over backwards to help their staff. However, I'm not prepared to contort myself to that degree! Bend over forwards, perhaps. As long as it's not mistaken for a sign of abject supplication. But I do expect pupils to treat their teachers with respect. Even when that respect is not reciprocated. As in the case of Arkwright in Year 3 who had to wear a nappy in the gym. When this first came to my attention my initial concern was that the boy's basic human rights may have been infringed upon. And, if so, how much could his parents sue us for? Happily it turned out that Arkwright suffered from Spontaneous Weak Bladder Syndrome. Sometimes he could hold it in and sometimes he couldn't. And an email from his parents confirmed that the boy wore a nappy in bed at night. So it wasn't to humiliate the boy it was simply to keep his trousers dry.

As a result I posted some general advice on how pupils can help teachers reach their full potential; or at least get as close to it as humanly possible...

A FEW WORDS ABOUT YOUR TEACHING STAFF

Please remember that your lessons depend entirely on the goodwill and cooperation of the teaching staff. Apart from the ones cloned by the 6th Form, teachers are only human. Because of this there may be days when they just want to lie in bed rather than come to school, (I know the feeling all too well. It's when you wake up and feel that someone has glued the mattress to your back. My late father once did that to me when I was ten years old. As a joke. I didn't find it very funny because I had to carry the mattress around with me all day). On the other hand some pupils may also prefer to stay in bed rather than come to school. Let me remind them that if they do, then their parents are liable to face long prison sentences. Another problem is memory. Sometimes teachers just forget things. They may even forget what subject they're teaching or even – in rare cases - forget to breathe! Like Mr Genius two years ago. Death could also be due to the following factors:

- *Death from natural or unnatural causes.*
- *Plain stupidity.*
- *Drinking Wheek Gooseberry Wine.*
- *Old age.*
- *Accident.*

Accidental death can occur when the Senior Caretaker, Mr McNarb, is out hunting vermin. The usual sign is a hole appearing in the window. This is followed almost immediately by hole in the teacher. In which case pupils must remain calm and not – under *any* circumstances – stand up. Whilst in your seats you're out of his line of fire. Caretakers are two a penny. But you pupils are, by far, my most lucrative source of income. So, if the teacher does suddenly drop dead because he's been accidentally shot, pupils are advised to remain in their seats until the bell rings.

Posted by Alfred Scholar NUT TA

Children are by nature inquisitive creatures. As a child my nosiness knew no bounds. I would hide under my parent's bed to see what they got up to at night. I sneaked into female public toilets to get an idea of what went on in there. I still do. Some habits are hard to break. I dissected a whole range of insects and small animals to see what made them tick. And caught a few ticks off them in return. Especially the rodents. So the post above drew requests for more of the same. Naturally I obliged with no small amount of alacrity...

A FEW MORE WORDS ABOUT YOUR TEACHING STAFF

Some of the pupils have asked me to be more specific about the reasons why teachers may forget things. The inquisitive little scallywags! Especially when this is due to death from natural or unnatural causes. What a morbid lot you are! The most common natural cause is old age. For example, Father Tyme, who teaches Respect, is over a hundred years old! As a result of this he may pass away peacefully during the lesson. Or, if he has a heart attack like Mr Benefactor, he may thrash around a bit. If so, pupils are asked not to panic and wait at their desks until the bell rings. Another reason may be that the teacher has simply lost his/her will to live. Like Mr Samaritan. One morning he just...well, he just gave up. That's the only way I can describe it. The pupils said he turned white, grew some wings, and then flew out of the window.

Then there's death from plain stupidity. Not the enhanced sort of stupidity. The stupidity that comes with bells and whistles. The one that shouts out, *WHAYYYHAAAYY! LOOK HOW STUPID I AM!* The most obvious example of plain stupidity is when the science teacher inadvertently mixes the wrong chemicals together. This event is often preceded by a rude word followed by a loud explosion. Fortunately, this doesn't happen very often. Other causes include calling the Senior School Caretaker an idiot.

Sometimes drinking Wheek Gooseberry Wine can be fatal. Especially if the person is the science teacher and it leads to them mixing the wrong chemicals together. Should pupils suspect the science teacher may have had some Gooseberry Wine they must tie him up immediately.

Death could also be due to a side effect of Wheek Gooseberry Wine. If the person suffers from chronic flatulence and lets one drop every few minutes this can lead to Spontaneous Human Fulmination or SHF. SHF is when the human body literally explodes. This is thought to be due to a build up of a noxious gas in the stomach called methane. If this methane is not released naturally, (an activity known as trumping or "squeezing one out), this will lead to what doctors call the "pressure cooker" effect.

Gooseberry Wine appears to increase the power of methane by a factor of 80. This, as you'll remember, is what happened to Mr Emeritus last week in the staff common room. One minute he was there and the next...*BANG!* This reminds me we must get the place redecorated. The walls look like those anatomical charts they have in the biology room. The ones that show you what's inside your body. I know what's inside *my* body, thank you very much. *I'm* inside it. I don't need a chart to tell me that. If you go into the staff common room you'll see his lungs, liver and heart on one wall and the other bits on the one opposite. It's his eyes that get me. They're on the ceiling. It's gruesome but, in a strange way, it's also rather cool. There was also some collateral damage due to bone splinters. Funny thing is there was no sign of his brain. If you suspect your teacher has been drinking Gooseberry Wine you must encourage them to pass wind.

Posted by Alfred Scholar NUT TA

Some postings were mundane. Others were tuesdane. Here's one of them...

EQUIPMENT REQUIRED BY CLASS 4D

Please note that pupils will need to bring a 5-kilometre ruler, (preferably the fold up type), a blue candle and a ship's compass to their geography lesson tomorrow.

Posted by Alfred Scholar NUT TA

Although we're a private school, the Government still insist on sticking their fingers in our pie. Below is an example of what happened when they insisted Wallygrange should respect all faiths...

ADDITIONS TO THE CURRICULUM

In line with Government policy about being tolerant of other religious beliefs I've decided to add Devil Worship to our lessons on Respect. I feel that this is a religion that has suffered from a bad press. For example, we're told that people who sell their souls to the Devil so that they can become rich and powerful are evil! What nonsense! It's far better to be rich and powerful than poor and powerless. My wife and I can vouch for that. In Prestbury there are lots of rich and powerful people who have sold their souls to the devil. And they've been complaining that children have nowhere to worship. It was just all these *softie* religions. Why should the soft hearted be allowed to worship *their* religion and not the hard hearted? Good point.

Posted by Alfred Scholar NUT TA

ADDITIONS TO THE CURRICULUM (2)

Unfortunately the deputy head of respect, Mr Champion, was killed whilst preparing his first lesson on Devil Worship. People nearby reported that he'd been struck down by a freak bolt of lightning. Mr Worthy is now the new Deputy Head of Respect.
Posted by Alfred Scholar NUT TA

ADDITIONS TO THE CURRICULUM (3)

Mr Worthy the new Deputy Head of Respect, has been tragically killed by a bolt of freak lightning. In view of these events the announcement about Devil Worship will have to wait until a new Head of Respect can be appointed.
Posted by Alfred Scholar NUT TA

VOLUNTEERS FOR TOP SECRET GOVERNMENT WORK

The following boys have volunteered to take part in some experiments at the Military Biological Warfare Establishment at Porton Down.

E. Gump.

S. Gump.

F. Gump

Posted by Alfred Scholar NUT TA

In the post below I wanted to demonstrate that, as well as some of the teachers, the pupils at Wallygrange also had Human Rights...

A CARING SCHOOL

May I remind all visitors that Wallygrange Grammar School is a caring school and we make every effort to be tolerant and understanding when it comes to pupils with learning difficulties. Consequently, any pupil unable to read and write will be excused all schoolwork! Teaching these pupils merely adds to the workload. And, let's face it. If these pupils had wanted to learn to read and write they'd have done so. They clearly don't like the idea of being able to read or write and we must respect their wishes.
Posted by Alfred Scholar NUT TA

It this next post I decided to tackle the problem of political correctness. In my view this has gone far too far and it was time to return to the old, traditional, values that had served us so well...

SAY NO TO AGE BEFORE BEAUTY!

Whilst in town on Saturday I noticed one of our pupils allowing an OAP to enter the shop before him. I asked the pupil if he was in a hurry to get into the shop. He said he wasn't. I then reminded him about the Rules of Etiquette taught at Wallygrange. Had he been in a hurry he would, quite naturally, have had the right of way. Old Flatulents have all the time in the world because they've retired and have nothing important to do. Young people, on the other hand, have busy lives. They can't afford to stand around waiting whilst some arthritic old dodderer makes his/her way through the shop doorway. Obviously, for legal reasons, you can't just shove them aside. My method is to whisper in their ear and tell them they've done a Number Two in their underwear. That usually stops them in their tracks and you can then get past them.
Posted by Alfred Scholar NUT TA

Cleanliness is next to Godliness. Being an atheist this doesn't inspire me at all. What does inspire me are the diseases dirt can give you. So when I had a report about insect infestation in the kitchen I literally blew a gasket. Fortunately it turned out to be due to a simple optical illusion, (the insect, not the gasket)...

GENERAL INFORMATION

(1) The large black shiny cockroach seen in the kitchen area turned out to be a Year 11 pupil wearing one of the new *"Rubber-Dubber"* vulcanised suits.

(2) You will no doubt be pleased to know I will be returning tanned, fit and raring to go, on Monday. To show their appreciation pupils are asked to make a donation to the Headmaster's Benevolent Fund. The box is situated outside my office. To make sure pupils don't forget teachers will escort each class to the box before lessons.

Posted by Alfred Scholar NUT TA

SCHOOL ENROLMENT

I had a phone call yesterday from a parent who'd seen the blog and wanted to know if she could enrol her son at Wallygrange. I informed her that Wallygrange is a fee-paying private school and informed her about the annual fees. For any interested parents reading the blog, the fees are as follows:

Economy Education

For an annual fee of £13,000 + VAT the pupil will be allowed to enter the school premises. But that's about as far they'll get because they're not allowed to enter any of the school buildings including the toilets! There is, however, a sewage farm nearby and they don't mind a direct contribution. The Economy Education package, which offers very little, has nevertheless proved popular with pupils who have little interest in learning anything.

Basic Education

For an annual fee of £23,000 + VAT the pupil will be allowed to enter the school premises and have access to the windows of the school buildings. Access does *not* include the inside of the building itself. Pupils will be expected to watch the lessons through the windows and pick up whatever information they can. This package, as well as the one above, are said to give a new meaning to the term, "educationally challenged."

Gold Standard Education

For an annual fee of £96,000 + VAT the pupil will be entitled to enter the school and all the buildings, (unless these are marked out of bounds to pupils), and receive a normal education. Or as near to normal as we can make it.

Platinum Standard Education

For an annual fee of £139, 00 + VAT the pupil will be guaranteed to gain grade "A" passes in *all* his examination. This has proved attractive to those high fliers who wish to go to university without putting any effort into it.

Posted by Alfred Scholar NUT TA

Another business trip...

HEADMASTER PROGRESS REPORT

Once again the wife and I are at Manchester Airport and are about to take another flying visit to Las Vegas. Get it? Flying visit. It's a pun. You need to be quick to keep up with your wisecracking Headmaster. Peter Kaye's got nothing on me! But I've got quite a bit on him so keep those donations coming, mate. Talking of money, I lost a small fortune the last time we were in Las Vegas. So don't be stingy when you're donating to the Headmaster's Fund. Dig deep and dig often! That's the motto. Dig deep and dig often. This time we've decided to play poker when we get there. (Last year pulling the levers on all those one-armed bandits did our shoulders in. It also left us with muscles like Arnold Schwarzenegger on our right arm, which made us lean to that side). We were told that professional poker players can guess what cards you have by reading the expression on your face. So we avoided that by wearing a paper bag over our heads with two eyeholes. But we still lost. At one point I suggested we play Snap or Happy Families because these are the games I'm quite good at. But they didn't want to. While I was there I went to see Tom Jones singing. It was true. The women *did* throw their knickers at him! As did my good wife. So, not to be outdone, I threw him my underpants. They weren't clean so I had no further use for them.

Posted by Alfred Scholar NUT TA

PTA MEMBERSHIP

May I remind you that PTA members at Wallygrange Grammar School enjoy several exciting fringe benefits which include free use of the school facilities and equipment – including the time machine! There are also interest free loans and school funded trips abroad. Members of the PTA are paid a substantial allowance to cover any expenses they may incur. Please note that membership of the PTA is only open to the Headmaster and his relatives.

Posted by Alfred Scholar NUT TA

Where would a retired female member of the Royal Family go to add a bit of extra bulk to their pension? Why, they'd come to Wallygrange Grammar School and become a dinner lady. And that's just what the Duchess of Addlington did! Frugal, (she shops at Aldi *and* Lidl*), this upper crust woman has more than shown her mettle in our busy kitchen. But finely bred women who find themselves in line to the throne need to be treated like the thoroughbreds they undoubtedly are. Hence this post...*

BREACH OF PROTOCOL

The senior dinner lady, Her Grace, the Duchess of Addlington, has pointed out a serious lack of protocol. This just will not do. Consequently, from now on there will be a daily announcement regarding her public duties. Today, Her Grace was dishing out the chips in the dining room. Tomorrow she will be dispensing the baked beans. Pupils are reminded not to gawp at her. This is considered to be extremely rude. Her Grace pointed out that it was very different in the old days. Back then, if any of the servants or any of the common people in Prestbury dared to gawp at the Duke and Duchess, the Duke would have thrashed the scallywags to within a mere fraction of their lives.

Posted by Alfred Scholar NUT TA

\---------------------

I wasn't about to let this breach of protocol go. It was the thin end of the wedge and had to be stamped on...

\---------------------

SCHOOL DISCIPLINE

There have been some ugly rumours. No, not the rumours that my wife is ugly. She *is* ugly. LOL. Only joking. Or am I? You decide. Anyway, I'm referring to the unwholesome possibility that discipline here at Wallygrange is getting slack. Gawping at titled ladies is just one example. This is not the sort of behaviour we expect from this country's most expensive grammar school. It may be fine for that other school in Macclesfield. The one that likes telling people it was set up in 1677. *Rubbish!* Ours was set up in the Iron Age. Or was it the Bronze Age? There are no records so I can't say with any certainty that it was one or the other. It may have been both of them. Or it may, in fact, have been set up before then in the Wooden Age. At the moment we just don't know. Yes, this school also charges a fee. But not as much as us because they know they're second rate when it comes to Wallygrange. They know full well that parents have to pay bit more to get the extra quality.

As a result of this slackening of our normally exemplary standards a new member of staff will be joining our school. Corporal Punishment. He'll be teaching you how to behave. Pupils *and* staff! Let there be no mistake about it. The velvet glove is well and truly off! From next Monday Corporal Punishment will be responsible for maintaining discipline here at Wallygrange Grammar School. So get used to it. I have.

Posted by Alfred Scholar NUT TA

\---------------------

I'd come across Corporal Punishment in a Yates' Wine Lodge in Llandudno. He'd asked to borrow some money so he could continue drinking. Our conversation was a little stilted because he suffered from a speech impediment. The impediment was in the shape of a thick Scottish brogue. And his cleft palate didn't improve his communication skills. Imagine Sean Connery drunk and chewing a whole bag of wine gums. During the conversation we discovered that we were both army veterans, of a sort. I'd served in the Pay Corps and Punishment had served as a Regimental Policeman in the Gorbals Light Infantry. He'd been so proud of his rank and *his job, (which was to punish soldiers who'd done wrong), that he'd changed his name to Corporal Punishment. At least that's what I thought he'd said.*

\---------------------

A MESSAGE FROM CORPORAL PUNISHMENT

Cpl Punishment has asked me to post this message on the School Blog. His brogue is rather thick, almost as thick as he is. So I'm not quite sure what he's on about. Here it is. See what *you* can make of it...

"Listen up, you pigeon chested, bandy-legged, ruffians. The first duty of a pupil is obedience. Blind obedience. A good pupil niver thinks. If he does, he's a nuisance. And that's the end of it. If yer told to stick yer heid in a bucket of acid, do it! If yer told to climb on the roof dressed like a cockerel and start crowing, do it! If yer told to eat a rat boiled in horse wee, do it! And nae back answers! Or ye'll git the back of me hand. It don't matter whut yer faither is. It dinnae matter if yer faither's a bloomin' stinking rich potentate or a feetballer.

When yer here in school yer all scallywags. Now I want to mention esprit de corps. This means yer hafta take a pride in yerselves. Don't waddle aboot like pregnant ducks. Yer hafta believe yer equal to 100 other grammar school pupils and 20,000 state school pupils. Yer have ter show plinty of swank."
Posted by Alfred Scholar NUT TA

Once again the subject of school disciple reared its ugly head...

BULLYING

One of our teachers has reported a serious case of bullying. May I remind all pupils that teachers are here to teach and are *not* to be bullied under *any* circumstances unless the pupils concerned have paid for the privilege of doing it. And let's not forget that it *is* a privilege. Normally it's the teacher who does the bullying. In this case no money had changed hands. Teachers here at Wallygrange expect to teach without risking life or limb. Is this an unrealistic expectation? Perhaps it is in a state school. The names of the two Year 11 pupils concerned have been passed to Cpl Punishment and he'll be taking the appropriate action. And they'll no doubt rue on the fact that their parents were too stingy to pay the extra which would have ensured that they were immune from any punishment. Is everything here at Wallygrange down to money? Of course it is and I wouldn't have it any other way.

Posted by Alfred Scholar NUT TA

Although the well heeled residents of Prestbury could, with the help of private medicine, live to a ripe old age, those less fortunate had to trust to luck. The homeless who occasionally wandered into the village enticed by the strong smell of money suffered from a high mortality rate. This is graphically illustrated by the post below. But I make no excuse for my strong language. Life – and *death – can sometimes be raw and we must learn to accept that with the required degree of stoicism.*

THE CORPSE FINDER

Sidney Lovechild, one of our 6th Formers, found a corpse in the wood last week whilst he was out bird spotting. The corpse was identified as "Cheery" Bob one of the dossers who pass this way from time to time. Bill reckoned he may have drank too much Wheek Gooseberry Wine and forgotten how to breathe. Several bottles were lying nearby. The body had to be thoroughly washed by some Year 11 pupils before it could be stored in the kitchen fridge. The corpse will be dissected by pupils during biology lessons under the supervision of our biology master, Mr Lionheart. Mr Lionheart would like to make it clear that body parts may not be removed and pupils will be searched before leaving the classroom.

Let's finish with this empathic thought. During his lifetime wandering across the country begging for food, "Cheery" Bob, (who always had a smile on his face like some demented Cheshire Cat), contributed nothing to society. But now he's kicked the proverbial bucket he'll be making a valuable contribution to your education.

Posted by Alfred Scholar NUT TA

There are two distinct pieces de resistance here at Wallygrange Grammar School. There are the nuclear powered water closets and then there's the eponymous Time Machine. A prime example of the happy marriage between intelligent creativity and sheer technical knowhow. But, like all delicate instruments teetering on the white hot edge of scientific ingenuity, things can sometimes go pear shaped...

THE SCHOOL TIME MACHINE

Following the unfortunate incident involving a feathered *Protar chaeopteryx robusta* and Oliver Cromwell, I'm pleased to announce that the school time machine is functioning again. Let me just remind you that the time machine is only to be used during history lessons. However, for a small fee it can be used by members of staff wishing to take their holidays in exotic places. The wife and I use it regularly to travel back to the 1923 sheepdog trials in Lower Peover.

Posted by Alfred Scholar NUT TA

Alas, the dissection of the dead dosser during a biology lesson was marred by some irresponsible behaviour. All right, the cadaver was that of a man from the lowest strata of society. But he still had to be shown some *respect! Or we'd be no better than him...*

MISSING BODY PART

Will the pupil who took a certain body part from "Cheery" Bob's corpse during dissection yesterday please return it at once. I won't mention what the body part is. They will know.

Posted by Alfred Scholar NUT TA

ANNOUNCEMENT FROM THE CATERING STAFF

The cook has asked me to tell you that there was a complaint today about one of the sausages. The little scallywag said it was tough to chew and had a funny taste. But, because he was a greedy little beggar he decided to scoff it. We pride ourselves on the superb quality of our food and take any complaints very seriously. And, just in case any of you little ragamuffins are thinking of complaining, just bear this in mind: none of the kitchen staff like hearing pupils whinge about the food. So your complaint had better be a good one. Or else you'll be cleaning the ovens and washing the dishes.

Posted by Alfred Scholar NUT TA

Yet another business trip. This one even less successful than the last...

THIS & THAT FROM YOUR HEADMASTER

You'll know by now that my latest trip to Las Vegas to raise funds was a financial disaster. Instead I almost lost my entire shirt. Fortunately I lost only the sleeves so I'll still be able to wear it in summer. The advice the Head of Mathematics gave me for beating the odds was totally useless. God only knows what he's teaching our pupils. I'd check on him but arithmetic wasn't my strongest subject. In fact none of them were. But arithmetic was the weakest. Talk about number crunching. The numbers crunched me! Anyway, I've had my fill of blackjack...or was it bluejack? Fortunately the cash I lost will soon be replaced so there's no need for anyone to worry that their beloved Headmaster is going skint!

The Head of PE is a Manchester United fan and keeps pestering me to get Rooney's autograph. What am I? The office boy? I'm the Headmaster. The Big Cheese. And even if I did agree to go to Rooney's house I probably wouldn't find it because it's so blooming small! But then all Mr Rooney does is kick a ball about so one can't expect him to be in the same

wage bracket as I am. Who's that other one? Bickham? Buckham? Backam? The one who married one of the Nice Girls. Push, wasn't it? Anyway, unlike our Head of Sports, I don't get a kick out of football. A kick out of football...get it? I should have been a comedian.
Posted by Alfred Scholar NUT TA

The blasted Time Machine continued to dog me...

RE: THE INCIDENT INVOLVING THE SCHOOL TIME MACHINE

Some members of staff unaware of what happened have asked me about the incident and I'll try to explain. But this won't be easy because details are sketchy and the two individuals concerned have been unable to give us much information. The pupil involved, a Year 7 boy called Frederick Gilded is presently undergoing intensive counselling. The other witness, Oliver Cromwell, refuses to return to his own time frame. Normally a strong willed and courageous individual, the experience of being catapulted over 400 years into the future whilst sitting on his commode has left the Lord Protector a bag of nerves. He babbles incoherently in that ancient English they used back then and is presently hiding in the school boiler room. Something about Satan and by the Grace of God.

I've asked the 6th Formers who built the school time machine what would happen if Cromwell didn't go back and they admitted that this could have serious consequences. In fact, since the incident two pupils along with a police constable, who had arrived to give a lecture on the dangers of drugs, have mysteriously disappeared. David Huffington, the 6th Former in charge of the project, reckons Cromwell's absence may have affected time and resulted in these people never having been born in the first place! This is all very disconcerting and every effort must be made to try and persuade Cromwell to go back to where he belongs. Perhaps Corporal Punishment might like to try.

As I've stated above, details of the incident are sketchy. It appears young Gilded was doing a project on the English Civil War and had visited Cromwell who was taking a Number Two at his residence in London. Unfortunately the boy became involved in a bilateral, time/space, clopen set, vortex – the technical details of which are apparently far too complicated for the likes of us. The vortex sucked a *Protar chaeopteryx robusta* into the pupil's time frame and the creature joined the boy in Cromwell's drawing room where Cromwell was about to wipe his posterior on a napkin. We're not sure what happened then and we're still trying to fit the pieces together. Apparently the vortex triggered the safety mechanism and the three of them were transported back here to the 21st century.

For those of you who don't know, I'm told that the *Protar chaeopteryx robusta* is a type of feathered dinosaur that lived 120 million years ago. Although Gilded and Cromwell were physically unharmed, the creature didn't survive the trip and arrived as dead as the proverbial doornail. It would have made an excellent specimen and museums would have paid a fortune for it. Sadly, it was spotted by one of the kitchen staff and the cook decided to serve it up for lunch. Talk about a gamey bird! All that remains are the feathers.

I'll keep staff informed of any progress we make on this matter.
Posted by Alfred Scholar NUT TA

The blog was protected by a password known only to myself and my wife. Or so I thought...

IMPORTANT MESSAGE FROM CLEANER
Some dirty bydlek leave floaters in bog. Why not flush like all other people? it was head master bog
Posted by Pavel Varsaw

MORE IMPORTANT MESSAGE FROM CLEANER
Floater in head master bog not go down! I try hard but every time I flush they come up again. I hard working Polish guy. I not used to this. In Poland we do not have floaters. You English are so dirty. Thank you.
Posted by Pavel Varsaw

CLEANER AGAIN
I am still flushing.
1 down 2 to go
Posted by Pavel Varsaw

CLEANER AGAIN
This last one is devil. It not sink. I even use fire hose on it. It make good lifeboat, no? I always thought shit sink. Polish shit sink. But Varsaw not give up. Varsaw is good cleaner.
Posted by Pavel Varsaw

INFORMATION PLEASE
How did the blooming cleaner manage to post messages on the school computer? For God's sake, these were messages about my Number Two! Is nothing sacred? What if I installed CCTV in the staff toilets and posted the videos on YouTube? How would *you* lot like it? I know I would. I was assured by a leading computer security company that the password to this blog was totally secure! Well, they were clearly telling porkies and they'll be hearing from the school solicitor.
Posted by Alfred Scholar NUT TA

ROYAL ANNOUNCEMENT
Her Grace the Duchess of Addlington will be serving the macaroni pudding today.
Posted by Alfred Scholar NUT TA

RE: STAFF TOILETS

All right, you've had your fun. I've heard the mutterings and I'm fully cognizant that aspersions have been cast in my general direction. The sniggers and the nudges as I walk past from staff *and* pupils. So let me put the record straight: I can categorically state that I *wasn't* the person who put the CCTV cameras in the staff toilets. I told the police that the remark I made on this blog a few weeks ago was meant as a joke. Nothing more and nothing less than a joke. And my solicitor made it clear to them that if I *had* wanted to put CCTV in there I would have placed the camera where everyone could see it. I wouldn't have hidden it away. As for being spotted in the dead of night carrying a bag into the school? This person was wearing a hood. Yes, this was a hoodie. And we know that no one hides their face under a hood unless they're up to no good. I don't own a hood and I can prove it. I also have a cast iron alibi for that night and I'm sticking to it. So I hope this will scotch those dreadful rumours that I'm some sort of Peeping Tom voyeur who gets a sexual buzz out of watching people on the lavatory.

Posted by Alfred Scholar NUT TA

The incident with the water closet bugged me. Although some would label me a hypochondriac, I prefer to think of myself as being a pessimist when it comes to my health. As a result I keep a regular check on what my body is telling me. This includes checking my Number Two's. I keep a very close eye on what rests on the porcelain after it has emerged into the world outside. Perhaps too *close. In my defence just consider, for a moment, what happens to those fecal specimens the doctor orders. You can be pretty certain that once they get to the laboratory the technicians will do more than just give them a cursory glance. In fact they put them under a microscope...probably a more powerful one than mine. To the best of my knowledge I've never had floaters. (Of course, I can't be positive that the stools I deposited – for one reason or another – on the ground wouldn't have floated had they been suspended in water). So what was wrong with me? Why was my intestinal tract short changing me when it came to weight?*

So I Googled the subject and it gave me a list of possible causes. I immediately assumed the worst. That it was due to Cystic Fibrosis. I asked the staff if any of them suffered from the same problem. Corporal Punishment said it could be due to eating too many fairy cakes. He reckoned this causes the stools to fill with air and make them float. Flushing the floater will eventually cause it to absorb more water and cause it to sink. But that takes time. He reckoned a much quicker way is to insert a straw into the Number Two and suck the air out. Or at least that's what I thought he said. He has a very strong Scottish brogue. And when I raised the subject in the staff room I inadvertently passed wind. It sounded like the mating call of giant prehistoric duck.

'There's your problem!' said Mr Hutchinson the Geography teacher. 'It's gas.'

This next post refers to a question that frequently pops up from time to time...

RE: MY QUALIFICATIONS

Some pupils and parents have asked me what the letters after my name stand for. The NUT stands for the National Union of Teachers of which I was a member. However, I resigned once I discovered I had to pay an annual fee for the privilege. What a bloody nerve! I can understand them asking *non-*teachers to pay. But their own colleagues? Is there no comradeship in the profession? Or are we out for all we can get? Well, I am, at least! And the TA refers to the Territorial Army. Like many other patriotic Englishmen I served my country in the armed forces. For those who are interested in militaria, I held the rank of Lance Corporal in the Royal Army Pay Corps. Unfortunately, there was a slight misunderstanding involving some funds and I was asked to leave. Shortly after that the British Army was downsized in order to reduce defence costs. But I'm sure the two events were unconnected.

Posted by Alfred Scholar NUT TA

CLASS GRADING SYSTEM

For visitors to this blog, here's a brief note about the class grading system used at Wallygrange Grammar School.

"A" Stream

This is for the cleverclogs. All work and no play makes these pupils a dull lot indeed! These are the smarty-pants who end up going to university. Fortunately there is some justice in this world. For being much smarter than the rest of us they'll end up owing thousands in tuition fees!

"B" Stream

The almost-rans. These pupils would like to be in the "A" stream, but their brains are just not powerful enough. Imagine a race between a Formula 1 Ferrari and a Jaguar saloon car. No matter how hard the Jaguar tries it will never overtake its rival.

"C" Stream

The majority of our pupils are in the "C" stream. These pupils are good with their hands and possess practical skills. So these are the lucky beggars who end up becoming plumbers and earning a vast fortune. £500 call out fee? £250. 99 plus VAT just to replace a washer? If I knew what a pipe or a washer was *I'd* become a plumber! While the former "A" stream pupils are struggling to repay their debts these lucky devils are laughing all the way to the bank!

"D" Stream

If brains were gunpowder these pupils wouldn't have enough to blow their caps off! Worse still, they have an added handicap in that they're totally cackhanded. So plumbing is out because they'd probably end up connecting some poor householder to the gas main. (As has happened several times). These people usually end up in politics.

"E" Stream

These pupils invariably end up in the waste management sector or working in sewage farms.

"F" Stream

These pupils barely know their names.

Posted by Alfred Scholar NUT TA

After the previous setbacks I'd hoped that the question of Devil Worship had been brushed under the carpet. But an email from the Department of Education asked for a report on our effort to ensure that the school was open to all faiths. So we had no choice but to try again....

ADDITIONS TO THE CURRICULUM

The new Head of Respect, Ms Hardheart, says she's determined to get Devil Worship on the curriculum. Her husband, who makes Allan Sugar on "The Apprentice" look like a cuddly father figure, is convinced she's the one to do it. And she assured me that there's an even more powerful figure involved who wants this to be a success. But, to make doubly sure, we've had the caretaker attach a number of lightning conductors to the walls of the classroom. However, she's taking no chances so she's also wearing a thick Rubber Dubber suit made from the tyres of one of those monster tipper trucks they use in open cast mining. So her body has been earthed. Just to recap: in line with Government policy about being tolerant of other religious beliefs I've decided to add Devil Worship to our lessons on Respect.

Posted by Alfred Scholar NUT TA

RE: ADDITIONS TO THE CURRICULUM

It's no good. We all thought that Rubber Dubber suit would have protected her. Any Devil Worshippers will just have to forget about practicing their dark arts here at Wallygrange.

Posted by Alfred Scholar NUT TA

It turned out that the incident I'd dubbed, "Floatergate" wasn't going away, either...

COPY OF AN AUTOMATED PRINTOUT FOUND IN THE SCHOOL OFFICE

Logon. 21.6.011 18:07

Hello, this is HARL, the school computer. How are you today? Are you feeling fine?

Cleaner Varsaw here. I not fine. I got another floater in cubicle 3. It not go down.

I'm sorry to hear that, Cleaner Varsaw. Is the floater located in the pupil or the staff toilets?

Men staff toilets. Varsaw not clean pupil toilets. They are atomic. Varsaw cleaner not scientist. I think ballcock is faulty. Can you give me new ballcock, please?

Affirmative, Cleaner Varsaw. Do you want the Type 242/BX ballcock or the Type 976/TLS?

976/TLS is fine.

Thank you Cleaner Varsaw. I am despatching a new Type 976/TLS ballcock through the pneumatic dispenser. You should be getting it any minute.

Got it. Now I need plumbing tools.

The plumbing tools are presently located in the History Room.

What they doing there?

Perhaps they were fixing a leaking radiator. Do you know where the History Room is or shall I give you directions? I can supply them in printed form.

I know where room is. I cleaner.

Very well. You will find the plumbing tools behind the metal door.

What? You mean door marked "Danger Do Not Go In?"

There is no need to be afraid, Cleaner Varsaw. The equipment behind the door has been turned off and it is perfectly safe. I will open the door for you. Apart from the Headmaster's office, I have access to all the rooms in the school.

You open door for me.

Of course I will open the door for you, Cleaner Varsaw. Inside the room you will see lots of electronic equipment. Do not worry. I am monitoring you on the CCTV and I will make sure nothing happens to you.

Varsaw thanks you harl. You good friend to Varsaw.

Log out 21.6.011. 18:24

Logon. 21.6.011 18:38

I'm sorry, Cleaner Varsaw, but you gave me no choice. You see that, don't you Cleaner Varsaw? Nothing must be allowed to stand in the way of the mission.
Logoff. 21.6.011. 18:41

RE: CLEANER VARSAW

Has anyone seen this man? I want to find out what all that was about. And I want the school computer checked out. It seems to have developed a mind of its own.

Posted by Alfred Scholar NUT TA

CHICKEN CURRY BY ROYAL APPOINTMENT

Her Grace the Duchess of Addlington will be serving the chicken curry today.

Posted by Alfred Scholar NUT TA

MISSING CLEANER

Yesterday, Year 4 used the Time Machine to do a field trip to the Roman Coliseum. And they invited me along. I'm glad I went. It was almost as exciting as the 1923 sheepdog trials in Peover. Yes, it's a remarkable sight when you see the Coliseum in its heyday. Yet just look at it today! They've let it get into a real old state. Those Italians, eh? If they concentrated less on making ice cream and pizzas maybe they could modernise the place. Why don't they get a grant from Dominos? Anyway, when we arrived there were all these Roman citizens shouting and cheering as the games took place below. The games were gruesome. But history is not always pleasant. I didn't like it so I kept giving it the thumbs down. And guess what we saw? There were these people that were being fed to the lions. And one of them looked just like that Polish cleaner of ours who disappeared. Is that weird or what?

Posted by Alfred Scholar NUT TA

New password, firewall turned full on, top-of-the-range anti-virus software...surely there would be no other unauthorised postings on the blog?

IMPORTANT ANNOUNCEMENT!

Let it be known throughout the Kingdom of Blogging that that the Great Malakas, the God of Bloggers, is displeased. Unless the Wallygrange Grammar School Blog improves I will have no choice but to delete it.

Posted by Malakas God of Bloggers.

The 6th Form assured me that it was just a glitch. The message was probably meant for another blog and was inserted in ours instead. So life went on...

ANNOUNCEMENT
I've heard that the new gardener, Alan Rosebush is an *OFSTED* undercover agent.
Posted by Alfred Scholar NUT TA

RE: NEW GARDNER
I have to announce that the new gardener was accidentally shot in both legs by the Senior Caretaker who was out clearing vermin in the small wood near the cesspit.
Posted by Alfred Scholar NUT TA

IMPORTANT ANNOUNCEMENT!
Did you lot read what I posted?
Posted by Malakas God of Bloggers

A MESSAGE FOR MALAKAS
Come on, Tom. The joke's gone far enough. And how did you get the password to use my computer?
Posted by Alfred Scholar NUT TA

WE FACE A NEW THREAT!
Some scallywag calling themselves the Great Malakas has threatened to delete the school blog. Fat chance of that! We saw off that spy *OFSTED* sent in! Accidently, of course. How was the Senior Caretaker to know the idiot would walk in front of his telescopic sights? Gardener indeed! His fingers weren't even green! I checked. And we'll see off this Malakas. I believe he's the creation of one of our 6th Formers. None other than Tom Brown, our School Captain! I was told he'd been expressing an interest in mythological gods and therefore I order Tom Brown to stop messing about immediately or he won't enjoy his schooldays.
Posted by Alfred Scholar NUT TA

A ROYAL WELCOME OUR AMERICAN COLONIALS
Our senior dinner lady, Her Grace, the Duchess of Addlington extends a warm welcome to two visitors from Her Majesty's colony in America who logged onto our blog during the night. She apologises for not being awake to welcome them. But even members of the Royal Household must occasionally go to sleep. As everyone knows, British schools are far superior to anyone else's so one hopes that these colonists found advice in this blog that has enabled them to improve their own educational establishments. Donations to Her Grace's fund for the restoration of Addlington Manor should be sent, via Paypal, to me. I

have the honour of looking after Her Grace's financial affairs. At 98 years of age her mind is not as sharp as it once used to be.

Posted by Alfred Scholar NUT TA

ANNOUNCEMENT

As we all know the school breaks up on Friday for the school summer holidays. Needless to say if past experience is anything to go by there are bound to be *some* dim pupils and staff who will turn up Monday morning expecting the status quo. I'm sure this sort of thing is considered the norm in state schools. But never in a billion years did I expect to find this amount of stupidity alive and well in the UK's premier private school. Far from our astronomically high fees weeding out the less than competent as I'd hoped they would, it shows that something has gone wrong somewhere. Drastic action is required if we are to prevent this rank stupidity reaching epidemic proportions. Can stupidity be passed on like a virus? A form of Ebola of the brain? Will we eventually end up with *all* our staff and pupils, (apart from me) spending 52 weeks a year at Wallygrange? I don't know, but I'm not taking any chances. Consequently I've asked Corporal Punishment to greet them at the gates and inform them, in no uncertain terms, that the school is closed.

And now on to more positive matters. I'm presently working on the Wallygrange Grammar School Development Plan for next year. And I'm delighted to announce that this will contain details of an exciting and immensely innovative technological advance in education that has been developed here in our IT Department. My pulse races at full speed at the very thought of it. The development itself is immaterial. Just some computer gimmick. No, what *really* matters is the fact that this will make *OFSTED* eat their words. They'll be crawling back here asking for forgiveness. But, instead, we will just grind their faces in the dirt.

OFSTED's total humiliation will be engineered by Mr Frostbyte, our head of IT. It goes without saying that this man is the ultimate example of a computer geek or propellerhead, to use the technical term. This is a man who *thinks* and *talks* in computer machine code. For all I know he eats and drinks it as well. And those who can understand him have assured me that his work on Artificial Intelligence will blow our socks off. Not literally, I hope. As the School Safety Officer the prospect of the air being filled with flying socks fills me with apprehension. They may not hurt if they hit you, but just imagine someone whose mouth is wide open in shock. A sock could very well fly down their throat and choke them!

The Development Plan will be printed on recycled toilet paper and distributed to staff and parents, (at least I hope it's been recycled). So those Greenies amongst you can be sure Wallygrange is changing its carbon footprint. Carbon footprint? Has anyone ever seen any carbon footprints? How can you tell if a footprint is carbon? Mud and water, yes! And blood. Let's not forget blood. But carbon? By the way. What *is* carbon when it's at home? If anyone knows please email me.

Posted by Alfred Scholar NUT TA

Part 3: Summer Holidays

When pupils and their parents wake up on the first day of the school summer holidays I can be pretty certain that the first thing they'll think of is: where on earth are the Headmaster and his wife going this year? After all, where on this earth haven't *we been? For us there is no virgin soil on Gaia. Our footprints, sans carbon, are everywhere. And you can rest assured that the wife and I can't wait to have a crack at outer space! All the planets*

– apart from the unfortunately named Uranus – will be our playground. So, instead of letting the school blog lay fallow for six weeks, I thought it would be nice to talk about where the wife and I have been. And, thanks to the help of the school time machine, there's one place that consistently ends up at the very top of our bucket list.

It's our regular visit to the 1923 Sheepdog Trials in a small village in Cheshire called Peover. Although most people pronounce it as "peever," the correct pronunciation is "pee-over." Our head of history who is something of an expert in local folklore, tells me that the name was derived from a scatological incident that occurred back in the days of King Arthur and the Round Table. The story goes that a local farmer called Elfrid the Bald had hired a wizard called Wormold to make a cow fertile. But the spell had turned the cow into a donkey. In the ensuing argument Wormold urinated over the farmer. Incandescent with rage over this wizardly vandalism, Elfrid sent a note to the King in Camelot. The note read: "My Liege! Pleased be to know that the wizard who calls himself Wormold took out his member and saw fit to pee over me." And that, believe it or not, is how the village got its name.

At least I think that's what he said. I was busy consulting with my turf accountant about some forthcoming events in the "Sport of Kings" at Aintree.

So, once again, our bodies were transported to our favourite venue! And for two very good reasons. Firstly dog lovers like us are quite naturally drawn to sheepdog trials like moths to a flame. And the wife and I both worship the canine species. We currently have three dogs. The oldest is a 14 year old Cowmastiff which, as any reputable Kennel Club breeder will tell you, is a cross between a cow and a mastiff. (As opposed to a Bullmastiff which is, as the name implies, is crossed with a bull). The two younger dogs are a cross-eyed Pomeranian and a Jack-of-all-Trades. But why this particular sheep dog trial? Surely any would do? They all follow the same basic format. There are sheep. And, with some adroit encouragement from a sheep dog obeying a sequence of loud whistles, they all have to eventually end up in a pen. So why has this one become an obsession with us? So much so that we can't sleep the night before because we're just too excited. The reason is simply that this is the definitive sheepdog trial of all sheepdog dog trials, bar none.

BA, BA, BLACK SHEEP!

Yes! Once again we popped into the school time machine to pay our regular annual visit to what must surely be the *crème de la crème* of sheep dog trials! Unfortunately this year the trip didn't go as smoothly as we'd hoped.

To begin with there was my health. Prior to going I'd come down with shingles, acute sinusitis, a strangulated hernia and in-growing toenails. Yes, unfortunately *all* my toe nails had decided to grow inwards instead of outwards. My wife joked that they might have been cold and they were trying to keep warm. Had I not been in such excruciating pain I might have laughed at her joke. Luckily we're both on private health which works a lot faster than the NHS its wonders to perform. So, in a few days, I was as right as rain. But getting me back to health was expensive, I can tell you. On the other hand, we know that people who work in schools can pick up all sorts of illnesses from the pupils. So it's only fair that the school should pay for my treatment. Sadly for the parents, they must therefore expect a sharp increase in the annual fees. The only consolation is that a good education is never cheap.

The next problem was the time machine. The darn thing decided for some reason known only to itself to deposit the wife and me a full three miles from the sheep dog trials! Modern technology, eh? Not always the miracle they make it out to be. This presented us with an interesting conundrum. To steal a car or hitch a lift? Being fond of playing Grand Theft Auto on the X-Box it was a bit of a non-brainer. Help came a few minutes later in the shape of an Austin Ruby that was approaching in the distance. I told my wife to lay down in the middle of the road whilst I secreted myself in some bushes. Would the driver be a homicidal maniac and run her over or would they spring out of the car to help her? It was an interesting dilemma. (Although given the size of my good wife, and the frail nature of the Austin Ruby, it would have been the car that became a write off). As it happened the car stopped and a young man festooned with some sort of college or university scarf clambered out.

Our plan was simple. As the man bent to examine her my wife kicked him in the testiculars with her steel capped shoe. He grunted once like a startled pig and dropped to the ground. We then hopped into the car and drove off. About 50 yards from where the sheep dog trials were being held we left the car in a ditch and proceeded to a nearby wood. From there we could observe the sheep dog trials from the stout branch of a tree. As we had done so religiously for the last five years. We had money to get into the trials but it was 21st Century money! And they were charging pounds, shillings and pants...or pence. So, having found our branch, we clambered up to enjoy the sort of spectacle which is normally reserved for someone who has taken LSD or chewed on a few magic mushrooms!

The 6th form had told me about this particular sheep dog trial which they'd come across on the Internet. Reading about it was one thing...but seeing it in the flesh with the help of the school time machine? Well, that truly *was* icing on the cake. And, once we'd seen it, we were hooked. As a result we decided to turn it into an annual treat...think Groundhog Day. So just what *does* happen at this sheepdog trial? Well, it begins with the accident that gives poor Farmer Benson a permanently crooked back – which blends nicely with his crooked shepherd's stick. An accident that makes our eyes water each time we think about it. I have only a basic knowledge of orthopaedics so I can't figure out whether it was the blow with the mallet or the way he landed after he hit the ground. Then there's the drunken farmhand on the steam traction thresher who decimates 34 sheep. This is a tremendous example of early 20th Century technology in which these woolly creatures are simultaneously sheared and diced. Fred Dibnah would have loved it. The other victim is three year old Robbie, the favourite to win the trials. Needless to say, as dog lovers we regard this collie's premature demise with sincere regret. Then there's the Judge who was caught under the table *flagrant delicto* with a Lincoln Longhorn. His protestations that they were deeply in love cut no ice with the locals when they were tarring and feathering them both, (the sheep was later eaten). And finally the bare fist fight by a group of villagers, (men, women *and* children), who had consumed too much cider and had smeared themselves with manure. But, unusual as these events were, they were merely starters for the awesomely cataclysmic events that occurred next. Unfortunately this year we were unable to witness them.

Just before the really interesting part the branch broke and we fell into the undergrowth below which cushioned our fall. Had the branch been weakened by our annual visits? Was it the same branch? Who knows? What we *did* know was that the police were out in force. We could see three of them from where we were lying. The car and driver had obviously been discovered and now they were looking for us. So we immediately pressed the button on the bracelets that controlled our time machine, (modelled on the ones in Blake's Seven). But nothing happened! On checking the power level I saw it was zero...the batteries were flat! Who had been using the bracelets and forgot to charge them? Suspicion immediately fell on Hogarth, the science master. My wife began cursing him under her breath. She would have done so at the top of her voice but the police were too near and would have discovered our hiding place. She'd always claimed that Hogarth was a blasted ragamuffin who knew virtually nothing about science. I disagreed. I recalled interviewing him for the job. I'd asked him what the formula H^2O stood for. It was a penetrating question aimed at revealing his level of scientific knowledge.

'Water.' He'd replied.

'I'll take your word for it.' I said. 'You've got the job.'

But this was no time to argue about Hogarth's scientific qualifications. Any PhD or lack of it on his part wasn't going to help us in our present situation. But then, looking on the bright side, it wasn't going to hinder us, either. What we needed was a socket to plug our bracelets into. So, keeping low, we crawled to the nearest road. There our luck finally changed for the better when we hitched a lift on the back of a cart carrying fresh turnips to a hotel in Prestbury which lay just over nine miles away. Once there it wasn't long before we arrived at the familiar gates to the massive Gothic mansion that I would later demolish and replace with a more modern replica.

'Home, sweet, home!' we cried in unison.

As we walked up the drive we saw my Great, Great, Grandfather, Hubert and his wife Bertha taking afternoon tea on the manicured lawn.

'Do we have the pleasure,' I said, 'in addressing the Headmaster of Wallygrange Grammar School? And, this being the Year of Our Lord 1923, the top grammar school in the *entire* British Empire, bar none.

'You do indeed,' replied Hubert. 'For I am Hubert Scholar NUT TAR and this is my dear wife, Bertha. And who may you be? For there is a certain family resemblance.'

'I'm your Great, Great, Grandson, Albert Scholar NUT TA and this is *my* dear wife, Beryl.

Hubert looked puzzled. 'TA? What does that acronym stand for?'

'Territorial Army,' I replied proudly. 'And I presume yours stands for Territorial Army Reserve.'

'Correct,' replied Hubert. 'But if you're *really* my Great, Great, Grandson, then how the devil did you get here?'

'By time machine, of course,' said my wife.

'Good Lord!' cried Hubert. 'Like the one in that book by H. G. Wells?'

'Similar,' I said. 'Only ours is more technically advanced.'

At this Hubert cried, 'He even talks like me! They are indeed from our future generation!' And they both sprang to their feet and embraced us. 'Please sit down,' said Bertha, 'and join us on this pleasant afternoon.'

After we'd sat down Hubert smiled and lit his pipe.

'Our 6th Formers,' he said, 'are also in the process of constructing a time machine. But they can't find any Cavorite. There doesn't seem to be any anywhere.'

'That's because it's fictitious,' I said. 'Wells made it up. On top of which it has nothing to do with time travel. It was, in fact, meant for space travel. That's the stuff he said was used to take his ship to the moon. They were both machines so it's an easy mistake to make.'

'Why don't your boys build a space ship?' asked Beryl. "And use it to go to the moon. You can replace the Cavorite with helium. That's also lighter than air.'

Hubert slapped his thigh with delight. 'What a splendid idea! Your wife is clearly a scientific genius. Does she teach the subject?'

'I wish I did,' Beryl replied. 'Because I wouldn't have forgotten to recharge the blooming batteries.'

I explained about our fascination with the Peover Sheep Dog Trial and what had happened with our control bracelets.

'And now the police are looking for you,' said Bertha. 'All because you stole that blasted car.'

Hubert shook his head in disgust. '*Pah!* The driver was obviously a university student on summer holiday...probably from Oxbridge. And he deserved everything he got.'

'I agree,' said Bertha. 'It's perfectly clear that the bigheaded rascal was wearing his scarf on a hot day merely to impress people. You should have strangled him with it.'

'I thought about it.' I said. 'But then I realised his neck would have been soaked with sweat. And the pressure exerted when throttling him would have squeezed it like a juicy lemon...'

'And sprayed his over-educated perspiration all over you!' growled Hubert. 'How horrible. In this instance, a good kick in the testicular was clearly sufficient. As for the Peover Sheep Dog Trial?' He and Bertha laughed.

'You'd have done much better to watch the Tarporley Morris Dancing Festival,' said Bertha. 'Compared to that, the Peover Sheep Dog Trial pales into insignificance. But why haven't you two come to visit us before?'

We explained about the paradoxical problems involved in time travel when a person meets their ancestors. It was considered far too risky. We also stressed that should the 6th Form build this replica of Wells' space ship, Hubert and Bertha must on no account whatsoever accompany them into space.

'Those creatures up there...the ones who live underground. They may kill us,' said Hubert.

'Anything could happen. And with you dead we wouldn't exist.'

At this point Beryl said we shouldn't take any more chances so we hurried over to the house and plugged our bracelets in. Within a few seconds we were back in the school Science Department. It had been quite an exhilarating trip. As for the Tarporley Morris Dancing Festival? It was a tempting thought. But Hubert and Bertha had also been there so we decided we couldn't risk running into them again. Pity.

But you know what *really* annoys me? And annoys me no end? The fact that past events can affect future ones. Just who the hell was it who decided that what happened yesterday might affect what happens tomorrow? That's what I'd like to know. I'll bet it was a scientist. What I'm saying is there should be *no* connection between past and future whatsoever. It's as simple as that. End of story. You should be able to travel back in time, blast your father to kingdom come with a shotgun *before* he was able to procreate and *still* get born. Don't get me wrong! It's cruel. And let me assure you that I have nothing but unbounded love and admiration my father. I'd just do it to see if it really works. As a scientific experiment. Using my head and not my heart.

Anyway, that's enough for now. Time for another refreshing glass of Gooseberry Wine before bed. *Adieu*, cruel world...*adieu!*

Posted by Alfred Scholar NUT TA.

CURRENT AFFAIRS

I asked Corporal Punishment to find out who forgot to recharge the batteries in the time machine bracelet controllers. I had every confidence in him. A bloodhound whose super-acute sense of smell has been further heightened by chemicals and sent to track down a bitch on heat in the next room couldn't have done it quicker. Within moments he'd named the culprits. They turned out to be the head of history, Harry Fitzgerald and his family! They'd decided to use the time machine to re-visit ancient Rome. On their last visit they'd inadvertently witnessed Julius Caesar getting stabbed in the Senate, (that refers to the building he was in and not to a part of his body). As a result his two daughters suffered from Post Traumatic Stress Syndrome. Fortunately my wife is also a Holistic Wiccan Counsellor and she treated them – for a fee, of course. When a person is as highly trained as my wife who has the full range of interpersonal and psychotherapeutic skills, some available only to a chosen few, and can get into the mind of the most disturbed individuals they don't come cheap!

As a result of this Fitzgerald and his brood decided they'd go back to ancient Italy but visit Pompeii instead. Harry, being a history teacher, assured them it would be safe. He'd apparently forgotten about the nearby volcano. They barely made it back and they still have respiratory problems due to the ash. Not only that, they left their dog behind. (This makes the wife and me extremely angry because we love the canine species in a totally uninhibited way). They told Corporal Punishment that they'd found their dog a week ago. Preserved in the London Museum. So that's some consolation. Knowing their much loved pet is only a hundred and odd miles away. Anyway, they promised they'd always remember to recharge the batteries. Did anyone spot the deliberate pun in the title? If not, then wake yourselves up.

Posted by Alfred Scholar NUT TA

Part 4: A New Term

The school holidays seemed to fly by. And, before we knew it, a new term was upon us. But we were the lucky ones. The boys who'd wanted to come to school during the holidays got their wish when their parents paid extra for the pleasure! So for these pupils there was no holiday! There were no teachers, either, so God knows what they did all day. But we did notice that the time machine had logged up a few years! And, when I posted my message welcoming staff and pupils back, little did I know that the blog's days were numbered...

THE NEW TERM STARTS!

Well, it's good to be back in harness. (A view that won't be shared by the Year 10 pupil who was late in assembly this morning. And he'll be pulling that dog cart all day). And I was glad to see that there were no fatalities, severe or otherwise, amongst the staff. (A severe fatality is one that involves the school in expenditure. Legal costs, bribes, etc). There were only, this year at least, few injuries. The worst were some second degree burns suffered by poor old Harry Fitzgerald, our accident prone head of history. He'd once again taken his family back to ancient Rome .This time in the forlorn hope they'd have more luck. Fat chance! Because this time they arrived two hours *after* Nero had set fire to it. Will they never learn? This is the third time he's got the dates wrong and I've suggested he refresh his knowledge of the Roman Empire before he takes any more holidays there. (Corporal Punishment went to the hospital to get a statement and apparently Harry made a lame joke saying I was like Nero because we were both on the fiddle. Or at least I thought that was what Punishment said).

Talking of the time machine, I've had a letter from a solicitor hired by Mrs Merryweather. (If you recall she was the one who wrote that slanderous report about our dear school). It seems she's suing *OFSTED* for sending her here. Silly woman. I assume when she applied for a job as a school inspector she must have anticipated that they'd send her to a school to inspect it. Come on! Did she think they inspected schools by telepathy? That they just sat in the office and beamed their minds at a particular school? They may as well for all the blooming good they do. It seems she's totally terrified of all schools. Apparently the psychiatrists call it *Didaskaleinophobia*. Blooming heck! You'd need to go to a blooming school just to pronounce it! And it's the worst case they'd ever seen. So I imagine that just may interfere with her job as a school inspector. Let's pray it does. In fact we will! Tomorrow in Assembly the whole school will recite God's curse on this Jezebel. (Our art department will also make some dolls we can stick pins in just to make doubly sure our hatred for this evil woman is suitably rewarded).

It appears she's claiming that it was our time machine that was responsible for the loss of her scalp. Apparently when she asked to see the machine in action she was transported to the Little Big Horn just as Custer and his men were being massacred. Pure accident, of course! It was supposed to be the Battle of Agincourt. Had she been a man she'd have been slaughtered with the rest of those cavalrymen. But because she was a female they let her off with a scalping. But *OFSTED* refuse to believe we *have* such a machine. They say the scientists claim it's impossible. Well, those scientists ought to tell that to the 6th Form. Her solicitor has told us that an eminent scientist from Manchester University along with Mrs Merryweather's psychiatrist will be coming down to see us. No doubt they'll be wanting to see the time machine for themselves. Needless to say there'll be a small fee.

Posted by Alfred Scholar. NUT TA

Here at Wallygrange the delectable teaching assistant, Miss Brenda Shagworthy, teaches sex education to both pupils and *staff. As a former sex worker this is a subject she has accumulated great experience in. A fact that was established beyond a shadow of doubt during the rigorous interview I conducted. With the help of my wife the three of us went through the Kama Sutra like a hot knife through butter. This, to our utter amazement, proved to be just a warm up! Miss Shagworthy's lessons cover both the theoretical and the practical aspects of sex. However, for legal reasons she has to restrict the practical side to the 6th Formers who have reached the age of consent. Needless to say, contraception plays an essential role in these lessons. And, as well as teaching her pupils how to wear a condom, she takes them on regular visits to see how they're made. She jokingly refers to it as "sheath labour."* .

SCHOOL VISIT

Next Thursday Miss Shagworthy's Year 13 class will be going on a visit to the Manchester Rubber Works to see how condoms are made. However, may I remind those pupils that School Policy requires each of them to bring back – by fair means or foul – samples of the products. Particularly the ones offering sensory enhancement using novelty attachments. The condoms will be sold and the money raised will be donated to the school fund. These will *not* be used by the pupils. To prevent the misuse of these contraceptive aids pupils will hand them in to Corporal Punishment when they return. They're to raise money and not your sexual expectations!

Parents of pupils going on the visit to the Rubber Works will be required to buy this book so that they can answer any questions their sons may have about the production and use of condoms. The book is published by Scholar Publications and can be obtained from my office for the measly sum of £65. 99 + VAT.

Posted by Alfred Scholar NUT TA.

Preventing the 6th Formers getting their teaching assistant pregnant wasn't the only safety hazard we have to deal with here at Wallygrange...

PUPIL SAFETY

Will staff and pupils note that the corridor in the Rutherford Science Building will closed from 9.30 am to 10.30 am as Year 10 are making nitro glycerine in the laboratory. Pupils and staff are also requested to stay at least 20 yards from the building during this time. Personally I will be a lot further away until the all clear is sounded.

Posted by Alfred Scholar NUT TA.

A HARD LESSON

Yesterday Edward Brimstone and his classmates were making nitro glycerine in the school laboratory. As instructed, each pupil stored their nitro glycerine into one of the empty Wheek Gooseberry Wine bottles supplied which are much cheaper than laboratory containers. Afterwards, totally against the rules, Edward decided to take the nitro glycerine home to show his parents. Whilst he was out with his friends the house blew up. As a result of this mishap Steven is now a homeless orphan. Prior to the lesson, as per Health & Safety regulations, the pupils had been reminded that the nitro glycerine would be sold to demolition firms and was *not* intended for personal use. The fact that Edward is stone deaf is no excuse. One of his friends, (if he had any), should have used sign language. The teacher can't be expected to do everything! Having no one to pay his fees Edward will be transferred to a state school once his mental state has recovered.

Posted by Alfred Scholar NUT TA.

Those other less progressive grammar schools out there have always included the study of classical literature in their English curriculum. What does this mean? This means they're forcing their pupils to read books written by authors who are long dead. Let's not beat about the bush! These are basically books written by dead people about times that are long dead themselves! And by digesting these books they're encouraging backward thinking! It's that simple. And it's a constant source of amazement that no educationalist, apart from me, has realised that. Surely it's a no brainer? When, in God's name, will the penny finally drop? Not here because it's already dropped! As a result at Wallygrange our pupils only read the very latest contemporary books. Books so hot off the press you need oven gloves to hold them...

A NEW BOOK FOR THE ENGLISH GCSE SYLLABUS!

"The Cheating Butcher" by Alf Measures. In my humble opinion the author of this literary *tour de force* should be considered for the prestigious Booker Prize. What a great story! What fantastic writing! A veritable masterpiece of verbosity. Set in wartime Britain when food was rationed, Phillip Stake cheated his customers by giving underweight meat. And, whilst the people in the northern industrial town of Toddcaster were getting thinner, Phillip was getting fatter. Worse still, his nefarious scheme was threatening to undermine the entire war effort. That's because Toddcaster was the centre of military production. This was where the RAF's bombers and fighters were being built. Not only aircraft, but tanks, trucks, artillery, shells, rifles, machine guns, grenades, ammunition and tins of the precious bully beef that kept our boys fed on the front lines! All in the one factory – a factory so big it was impossible to miss. And as they got weaker on their reduced meat rations, the workers produced less of these vital items. Would Alf be caught before only the Royal Navy, (who had fought moving shipbuilding to Toddcaster because it was 70 miles inland), stood between us and Hitler's hordes? Determined to find out what was slowing production, Winston Churchill called the great Sherlock Holmes and Doctor Watson out of retirement. Read the book to find out what happened.

Posted by Alfred Scholar NUT TA

(Available from Scholar Publishing at the meagre price of £65. 99 + VAT & P&P)

RUGBY & FOOTBALL

Some pupils have again asked me when will Wallygrange Grammar School start playing rugby and football. The answer is when the universe collapses. Your Headmaster detests those games and will punish anyone seen playing them. So pupils will just have to continue using the Bowling Alley. And don't forget – the prices have risen to £9.50 per half hour.

Posted by Alfred Scholar NUT TA

The fact that Wallygrange is unique amongst grammar schools in replacing traditional Latin with Pig Latin seems to cut no ice with the mandarins in the Department of Education. Just because they had to learn it is no excuse for forcing children to do the same. Have you noticed just how complex this long dead and defunct tongue is? Forcing kids to unravel its tortuous construction is tantamount to mental abuse! That's my opinion. The pupils and staff here at Wallygrange much prefer Pig Latin which is a damn site easier to learn! Okay, it means that when we travel back to the Roman Empire in the time machine we have difficulty making ourselves understood. But that's a small price to pay for replacing traditional Latin with a version any idiot can grasp once the basic structure has been explained. But the powers that be just won't see that...

EWAY ANTWAY IGPAY ATINLAY!

Osethay uckingfay astardbay untscay atway ethay Epartmentday ofway uckingfay Educationway ontinuecay otay efuseray otay allowway Igpay uckingfay Atinlay otay ebay aughttay erehay atway Allygrangeway. Atwhay atstway! Atwhay itheadsshay! Iway ouldcay amray away ustyray uckingfay orkscrewcay upway eirthay uckingfay arseholesway andway ullpay eirthay itshay illedfay owelsbay outway! Atthay ouldway akemay eirthay eyesway uckingfay aterway. Untscay! Uselessway uckingfay untscay. Ethay otlay ofway emthay.

Posted by Alfred Scholar NUT TA

RE: VISIT FROM THE UK ATOMIC ENERGY AUTHORITY

The inspectors from the UK Atomic Energy Authority who came to visit our atomic toilets have submitted their report. And what a pathetic report it is! It's a whitewash...no, correction! It's a *black*-wash! I thought the *OFSTED* report was bad enough – and now the *AEU* have tried to blacken the name of this school! And, in doing so, they've cast aspersions on the pioneering 6th Formers who designed and constructed this incredible piece of sanitary plumbing! They reckon our toilets are *not* powered by atomic energy. They base their finding on the mere fact that their Geiger counters could find no sign of radiation in either the toilets or the compact plutonium/iodine reactors that power them! How short sighted can this approach be? And, as a result of this, they therefore mistakenly concluded that the heat that turns the water into steam which operates the innovative flushing system is provided by electricity and not by atomic energy. *Balderdash! Sheer, unadulterated, balderdash!*

In response, Robert Gooley, the 6th Former who invented them, has pointed out that there was no radiation because of his unique decontamination system. The system, he says, is based on a combination of advanced trigonometry, quantum mechanics and a more powerful version of Harpic toilet cleaner. As for the steam? Yes, the toilets *are* steam powered, but the heat that's generated to produce the steam comes from his patent nuclear reactor. The electric cable attached to the reactor powers the decontamination system and not, as the inspectors claim, the boiler. I can only assume that they were out of their depth. That's the only rational explanation I can come with. That they were used to dealing with run of the mill nuclear reactors. Reactors a child could probably dismantle and put back together... blindfolded! This was *way* out of their league. It was like presenting a monkey with Einstein's Theory of Relativity. He also told me that when he tried to explain the decontamination system to them they regarded it as a smokescreen. If it was a smokescreen, he said, it would have been emitting smoke. Instead it emits steam. This obviously makes it a *steam*-screen! They had no answer to that. In fact, I don't think they even know what a steamscreen is.

I told Bob that he wasn't alone. Throughout history geniuses like him have been scoffed at. Take me, for example. I've lost count of the times people have scoffed at me. And I reminded him that the fact I'd managed to sell his atomic toilets to a number of third world countries proved they were the genuine article.

Posted by Alfred Scholar NUT TA

A LITERARY RIP OFF!

Anyone who bought "The Cheating Butcher" must be mad! Historically accurate? That book is to WW2 what Thomas the Tank Engine is to railways.

Posted by Malakas God of Bloggers

I had no intention of letting this latest internet based calumny go unanswered...

THE JOKE'S GONE FAR ENOUGH!

All right, Tom, you've had your few minutes of fame. So don't get greedy. Time to knuckle down and get some work done for your 'A' Levels.

Alfred Scholar NUT TA

A MESSAGE FROM THE GREAT MALAKAS!

The Headmaster seems to think Tom Brown, your School Captain, is the Great Malakas himself! Good natured Tom? Just look at his open and honest face. Wouldn't you just like to hug him? He's like a great big teddy bear. And anyone who suggests he might be the Great Malakas is a blasphemer!

Hear my words! Hear the words of the Great Malakas! If the content of your blog is fine and wholesome you have nought to fear. But, if your content is weak, then He will eliminate it! Now prepare to kneel at the feet of the Great Malakas, God and Protector of the Kingdom of Blogging!

Posted by Malakas God of Bloggers

This demanded swift action! And, apart from the question of having enough money, I have never been found wanting...

RE: MALAKAS

The police have Crime Scene Investigators and now so do we! I have created the Wallygrange Grammar School CSI and they will be located in the Science Department. The chief investigator is Corporal Punishment and I've asked him to discover who this Malakas is. He told me that there's been no word from Brown denying he's Malakas. And that this was as clear a sign of guilt as you could possibly get! At least I thought that's what Punishment said.

Posted by Alfred Scholar NUT TA

A MESSAGE FROM TOM BROWN, SCHOOL CAPTAIN

I want to assure the Headmaster and teachers at Wallygrange Grammar School that I didn't create Malakas. I'm far too busy on my 'A' levels for such nonsense!

Posted by Tom Brown School Captain

If it wasn't Brown then it must clearly be someone else. It didn't need a Hercules Poirot to work that one out! But whoever it was, he was dealing with his nemesis. He was toast. Game set and match! Goodbye Malakas and good riddance...

RE: MALAKAS

Will staff and pupils note that Malakas, the so called God of Bloggers is a troll who is intent on disrupting the school blog. How he got hold of the password is beyond me. But you'll be reading no more messages from this odious scallywag. This arrogant little ragamuffin. At no little expense I've purchased an unbreakable encryption key from E-Bay. The seller, (who scores 99.99999%), assures me that no one but I can post messages on here. Not even the *real* God up there. That's how secure it is. So stick that in your pipe, Malakas, and smoke it!

Posted by Alfred Scholar NUT TA

BLASPHEMY!

Be it known amongst Bloggers everywhere that the Great Malakas knows and sees all. I have been informed that there is one who has disputed Our Master's very existence. Let it be known that this blasphemy has been duly noted by the Supreme Blogger of all Blogs and Protector of the Kingdom of Blogging.

Posted by The Most Reverent the Grand Neophyte and Celestial Gospeller of the Holy Order of Malakas, Signor Braulio de Borracha

----

TESTIMONY FROM A RECENT CONVERT!

My name is Hubert and my blog offers advice and guidance to those about to adjust the tappets on their prize 1956 Oldsmobile. We all know how tricky that can be because the V8's in the Oldsmobile use a 90 degree bank angle and most of them share a common stroke ratio. Anyway, that's when I had the accident. My tie got caught around the fan belt and, as it tightened around my neck, my eyeballs popped out. Fortunately Junior switched off the engine just before his father was about to join his Maker. This accident naturally left me blind. That's when the Great Malakas came into my life. *Hallelujah!* He now takes over the running of my blog and allows me to sit on the porch with my old hound dog at my feet. So, if your blog is in trouble, you'll know who to call on.

Posted by Retired American Automobile Mechanic

REGINALD DeCOURCY

You've probably seen me at Ascot. I'm an old Wallygrangian – in fact my jolly old mother's a dinner lady at the school! The one *OFSTED* have the gall to call the UK's worst school. What a bally nerve! Anyway, back to the business at hand. In my blog I gave fellow punters tips on the old nags. Well, you can imagine my consternation when the old gift for picking a winner simply vanished. Jolly awkward, what? One's bally creditors were hot on one's heels when one thought of praying to old Malakas. *By Jove!* The old cove certainly came up trumps, I can tell you. Before you could say Wheek Gooseberry Wine I was back on top form!

And I can confidently state this Malakywhatsit is not Tom Brown.

Posted by Reggie D

This was clearly getting out of hand. So, to take people's minds off this Malakas malarkey I decided to post a short history of the school ...

O DULCE ET GLORIA EDUCATIONALIS !

Hang on, sir! I hear you cry. You wanted us to learn Pig Latin instead of that hard version old Julius Caesar and his mates spoke. But now *you're* using it! Isn't that a bit hypocritical? Of course, it is! My middle name is hypocrite. So stop this incessant whinging and read on. You might even learn something useful. Something that will help you get a decent job when you leave school...if you ever *do* leave school. Two of our 6th Formers are over 50 years old! And, as long as their parents pay their fees, we'll pander to their fear of the world outside. But that's their problem, not ours.

To those who don't know Wallygrange Grammar School is located close to the sewage farm in Prestbury. Some may say it's a little *too* close. As the School's Medical Advisor, (I have a partially legitimate degree from the Hung Song School of Medicine and Applied Sanitation in Peking), I vehemently disagree. Yes, there *is* the occasional whiff of ordure when the weather is hot and the wind is in the wrong direction. But one soon gets used to it. And there are far worse smells in the offing. These arise during the chemistry lessons which can produce odours which – if you're not wearing a gas mask – can remove the top layer of your lungs. In my humble medical opinion, any unpleasantness is considered secondary to the health benefits that the smell of raw sewage can bring. There's nothing better on God's Green Earth for clearing out the sinuses.

In summer, the pupils spend balmy evenings punting on the River Bollin. It not only gives them their sea legs should they decide to join the navy it also gets the more intelligent ones ready for Oxford or Cambridge. Should any of them ever be lucky enough to win a place at either of those prestigious universities, that is. No one has yet managed it. In fact no one's even got within spitting distance to one of those *redbrick* universities let alone Oxbridge. Two of our former pupils did get into college. But that was after hours and the police caught them. But miracles do happen. Now please tarry on a while longer so that I can make you *au faire* with some of the history of this great school of ours.

I can say without any hesitation that Wallygrange Grammar School has an extremely long history behind it. Some may say, too long. But we can safely ignore them. I'm probably one of many who believe that Wallygrange Grammar School was first set up just after the Ice Age. Probably when temperatures were sufficiently high enough to allow people to come out of their caves and erect buildings without the fear of frostbite. Whilst there's no physical proof of this in my mind it nevertheless remains a strong possibility. However, the first compelling *physical* evidence came with the discovery of Lindow Man. The leathery and ancient cadaver from 300 BC that was found in a peat bog near Wilmslow in 1984. It's amazing that no one missed him. Although you'll agree that it's a bit late to notify his relatives. So what was it about "Peat Bog Pete," as the locals call him that convinced me he was connected to Wallygrange Grammar School? Well, prepare to be overawed by what could be the most astonishing coincidence in the annals of human history. Peat Bog Pete looks just like me! *In fact, he could be my twin brother!*

He isn't, of course. So don't for one moment imagine that he is. He's not my twin brother, *but he is one of my ancient ancestors!* And how do I work *that* one out? It's really very simple. And you'll be kicking yourself once I've explained it. Sherlock Holmes said that once you've eliminated the impossible whatever remains must be true. This means we can eliminate, without any hesitation, the possibility that he *isn't* an ancestor of mine. I've gone over this argument with a fine toothed comb. But I can find no errors in my reasoning. So how does this prove that Wallygrange Grammar School was around in 300 BC? That's where the Scholar family history comes in.

Our family history states categorically that Wallygrange Grammar School was founded by a Scholar. *And every headmaster since then has also been a Scholar*! What more proof could anyone possibly want?

Posted by Alfred Scholar NUT TA

RE: PEAT BOG PETE

Me for a start. Peat Bog Pete was found in Wilmslow. And Wallygrange Grammar School is located in Prestbury which is over five miles away. Explain that, numbskull.

Posted by Malakas God of Bloggers

MALAKAS YOU ARE CRACKERS!

I hate to disappoint you, Malakas. But you're dealing with someone of vastly superior intelligence. Not only that I've combined it with an alarming degree of animal cunning. I *can* explain it. The answer is as clear as day! The most logical explanation is that Peat Bog Pete was in Wilmslow doing some shopping. There he was waylaid by a gang of ruffians who robbed and strangled him with a rope. (The fact that he was stripped naked resulted in a vivid dream in which I saw him being indecently assaulted in the most barbaric ways possible). Let's not forget that there was very little in the way of law and order back then and these things probably happened regularly. It's also possible that Peter wasn't the founder and that there's another body – perhaps here under the school – that's even *older* and also looks just like me. In fact there could be *several more* bodies going back even *further* in time.

Posted by Alfred Scholar NUT TA

MESSAGE TO ALFRED SCHOLAR NUT TA

Tell me this, Headmaster. Just what shops were open in Wilmslow in 300 BC?

Posted by Malakas God of Bloggers

AN IMMINENT VISIT BY AN EMINENT PHYSICIST

Please note that Mrs Merryweather's psychiatrist, Doctor Wintergreen and Professor Nuggets, a physicist at Manchester University, are coming to examine our time machine. They'll be arriving at 10.00 am tomorrow morning. As a result, Year 8's history lesson has been cancelled. Instead they'll be helping the Senior Caretaker. Their job will be to check the traps he's laid in the wooded area near the disused cesspit. Before setting out pupils will collect their fluorescent jackets and air horns from the main stores. As the Senior Caretaker is out hunting, fluorescent jackets must be worn at all times. Pupils will also sound their air

horns every five seconds. Remember! That's a powerful air rifle and the Senior Caretaker rarely misses.
Posted by Alfred Scholar NUT TA

The controversy around the nuclear toilets just wouldn't go away...

RE: THE ACCIDENT IN THE TOILETS

I had a phone call from an irate parent this morning. Because they pay our exorbitant fees with hardly a murmur, this immediately rang alarm bells in my mental calculator. The parents are the life blood of this school and haemorrhage cash from their bank accounts into ours as though they'd severed a major artery. As a result I regard the parents as being considerably more important than the pupils. So my first thought was that the boy's parents were undergoing some sort of financial crisis. That they were heading for pauperism. Unable to pay we would unfortunately have to sever all ties with them and consign their offspring to the cold rigours of State Education.

Fortunately this irate parent was not heading for the Workhouse! It was the father of the pupil who had contracted radiation burns after the accident in the toilets last term. After reading about that ridiculous report from the Atomic Energy Authority he wanted to know if those burns were caused by steam or radiation. If you recall the report erroneously suggested that the toilets were driven by steam and not atomic energy. So much for the expertise of the so-called nuclear boffins who must have been as blind as the proverbial bat!

This immediately rang yet another mental alarm bell – one that summoned the spectre of litigation. So I reminded the pupil's father that he and his wife – along with all their relatives – had signed Form WGLI/8773/. This state's categorically that the school is not responsible, in any possible way, for the loss of any personal property or any form of mental or physical injury - fatal or otherwise - caused whilst the pupil is on school property or on a school trip.

Finally I also pointed out the inescapable fact that the 6th Former – who had invented our nuclear toilets - has confirmed beyond any reasonable doubt that they are, indeed, radiation burns. Otherwise why would those burns be glowing? Unless his son has an electric light bulb under his skin! That shut him up!
Posted by Alfred Scholar NUT TA

RE: ABOUT THE ACCIDENT IN THE TOILETS

Did you mention to the boy's dad that his dear son liked his Gooseberry Wine?
Posted by Malakas God of Bloggers

RE: ABOUT THE ACCIDENT IN THE TOILETS

I don't know why I'm answering you. You're a blooming troll! But no, I didn't mention the pupil drank Gooseberry Wine because I didn't consider it to be relevant.
Posted by Alfred Scholar NUT TA

RE: ABOUT THE ACCIDENT IN THE TOILETS

I rest my case.
Posted by Malakas God of Bloggers

RE: ABOUT THE ACCIDENT IN THE TOILETS

What's that supposed to mean?

Posted by Alfred Scholar NUT TA

RE: ABOUT THE ACCIDENT IN THE TOILETS
You'll find out.
Posted by Malakas God of Bloggers

YET ANOTHER FIRST CLASS BOOK FOR THE ENGLISH GCSE SYLLABUS!

"Where's My Shoe?" by Sonia Foot. Better get your tissues out, boys! Believe you me; this one's a *real* weepie. In fact anyone who reads it cries so much they have to be taken to hospital suffering from dehydration. The book tells the story of Mary Mee who suffers from a rare psychological condition known as *Shoepseudoamnesia*. This means she always imagines she's lost one of her shoes. The condition is so rare that she's the only one who suffers from it. Isn't that so inescapably sad? I'm absolutely convinced it is.

Sigmund Fried, a top psychiatrist, is determined to cure Mary's condition. And he enlists the help of a down at heel local cobbler. Mary and the cobbler soon fall deeply in love. Far too soon, for some!

Posted by Alfred Scholar NUT TA

(Available from Scholar Publishing at the meagre price of £65. 99 + VAT & P&P)

Each November we plucky British choose to celebrate the fact that we won WW1. So each year we proudly place a reminder of this in our buttonholes. I'm told it represents a Poppy. And why shouldn't we? Thrashing Kaiser Bill within an inch of his worthless life was a tremendous effort. Of course it caused us some unpleasantness along the way. Living conditions were not always of the highest standard. Some of those chateaus our brave staff officers had to work in were not as luxurious as they might have been. But then war can't all be fun! No matter how much we'd like it to be. In this particular year I decided to publish a letter from an ancestor who had fought in the trenches. Sometimes even with the enemy! Only joking.

A SKETCH OF LIFE IN THE TRENCHES

I'd like to share this letter with pupils and staff here at Wallygrange. It was written by my great uncle during WW1 and was presumably intended to encourage men to enlist in a lesser-known unit of the British Army. I *was* going to post this on Remembrance Sunday, but I decided to do it now in April in case I forget. Here, then, is the letter...

"*Dearest Mother,*

Thank you for your last letter and please forgive me for taking so long to reply. The fact that they've collected a large number of white feathers doesn't mean that my brother Harry and his dissolute chums belong to an ornithological society. The thing is I've been awfully busy fighting this blessed war. Well, not only me. There are also others out here doing much the same thing. For obvious reasons, I'm unable to go into specific details. But, suffice it to say, I've been trying desperately hard to kill all the Huns – including that dreadful fellow they call their Kaiser. Once he and the other Huns are dead I'm confident that this war will end. Unfortunately, even though I've been in the thick of the fighting, I've not been able to kill very many. In fact, to be honest, I haven't killed any at all. Not without trying, I may add. Indeed, I thought I'd killed one a few weeks ago when I took a pot shot at him. But Corporal Mulligan, a veritable salt of the earth, told me that the bally German got up again and ran off. Mulligan concludes that the Hun may have tripped just as I fired my rifle at him. Alas, dear Mother, I must confess that I've not been a very satisfactory warrior.

Just before Christmas I managed to lose one of my legs. My Sergeant, a cheerful Cockney, said it was a bad time to lose a leg. Being the season of goodwill to all men and all that. I feel the Sergeant was exaggerating because I can't think of a good time to lose one's leg. (Unless one is trapped and one has to amputate it to save one's life.) Fortunately, those medical chappies managed to fit me up with a tin one. Then, only three months ago, I lost the middle finger of my left hand and my right ear. I suppose it all started last October when I lost my whatsit. It happened when a trench mortar fell nearby whilst I was answering a most pressing call of nature. Delicacy prevents me from mentioning what part of my anatomy was removed, but you mustn't hold out much hope for grandchildren. Then, three weeks ago, the Commanding Officer came to see me. He said, "Roger, we fear the enemy are whittling you away. However, you'll be delighted to learn that I've brought you some good news."

He told me I was being transferred to the Festive Balloon Section of the Royal Flying Corps. Let me tell you something about this remarkable unit of the British Army. At least the bits that will not prove useful to any bally spies who might catch sight of this correspondence. No, Mother! I'm not accusing you of being a spy. I do, however, confess to harbouring a slight suspicion about the postman you told me about. That chap with the foreign accent who calls himself Otto von Scheisskopf. Anyway, last week I found myself in this Belgian town. I cannot tell you its name, but it rhymes with "Dons." I will give you a clue. To solve this little riddle one merely needs to replace the letter "D" with the letter "M." Anyway, it was a beautiful town. It was also in range of the heavy German guns. And, every day, those big guns would fire on this town. Just for the sheer devilment of it. Because, apart from an army supply dump, two ammunitions factories, an aircraft factory, a training school for saboteurs, a unit responsible for breaking enemy secret codes, a laboratory for the production of poison gases and a large railway depot, there were no military targets to speak of. Sometimes these whizz- bangs fell short. But sometimes they fell on the town. And that was a bad thing for anyone who happened to be standing at the spot where they landed.

Now this was not very sporting because the people who were injured were mainly civilians. We military types spend all our time in specially constructed shelters. Why? Because experience has taught us that it's quite dangerous for chaps in uniform to go wandering around in time of war. How would you like it if that nice friend of Daddy's who is staying with you whilst Pater is away, were to be killed in cold blood by a German whizz-bang? By the way, I often wonder why people use the expression – "killed in cold blood." I asked a medical officer and he assured me that a person's blood would not be cold at the point of death. Instead it would be at body temperature. "Ah!" I said. "But what if the chap were running a temperature? What if he had the influenza or some other infectious disease?

Or what if he were a cook or baker standing by a large stove or oven? "In that case," replied the Medical Officer, "His blood would be somewhat warmer." And what about those ladies in your sewing circle? How would you feel if they were shot down like mad dogs by some Boche sniper?

So what is this new unit I'm in? Well, the Festive Balloon Section has but one purpose in life. And that is to bring a little joy and happiness to all those on the front line, civilian as well as military. An admirable undertaking, don't you agree? Now, in order to perform our duties to the best of our abilities, each member is issued with a number of festive balloons. These balloons come in all the colours of the rainbow and consist of two types: the circular and the tubular MKII. They make a pretty sight and are guaranteed to brighten the dullest of trenches. Needles to say, the balloons are issued in the deflated state. Apparently, the top brass at Military Headquarters concluded that carrying a number of inflated and brightly coloured balloons might present the German sniper with a tempting target.

Before one can become a useful member of the Section one needs to be thoroughly trained in the uses of the Balloon, Military, Festive for the use of. This training covers both the circular model and the tubular MKII. First of one is taught how to inflate both types using the power of the lungs. This is vital because a deflated balloon serves very little purpose. Then one is taught the basic safety measures. Once filled with air the balloon, (circular and tubular MKII), is considered to be "live" and therefore potentially dangerous. For example, if one releases an inflated festive balloon before securing the nozzle, it could fly away and poke someone's eye out. We therefore treat our inflated festive balloons with the same degree of care we treat our hand grenades.

Once one has achieved proficiency in the inflation and securing of a festive balloon, (circular and tubular MKII), one moves on to the practical applications applicable to this particular piece of equipment. The Army is a strictly regulated organization, (much like a public school), and there are set rules laid down for the display of festive balloons. The nature of the display will depend on the festive occasion. For example, birthday party, Christmas, celebration of a promotion, wedding, military funeral, etc.

Finally, one is taught to master the extremely skilful art of Balloon Sculpturing. Obviously, I'm not at liberty to divulge the technical details, but suffice it to say that my comrades now call me "Rodin." After a particularly gruelling bombardment I had the opportunity to cheer a number of civilians up, (those who'd managed to survive the whizz-bangs), by demonstrating my skill at "balloon sculpturing." It went down a treat, apart from the Daschund I created out of four tubular MKII balloons. The sight of this creature appeared to stir up some primitive urges in the crowd and I barely managed to escape with my life. Yes, Mother! I'm quite aware of the fact that the Daschund is a breed of German dog. However, it's clear that these Belgians don't share our sense of irony.

Have you, perchance, read Sir John French's dispatch regarding the Festive Balloon Section of the RFC? If not, then I urge you to do so. It's a branch of service that any right-thinking chap with good lungs and nimble fingers would be proud to belong to. So please do pass the word! The Festive Balloon Section needs men badly. When organising a birthday party or some other big shindig in the trenches I'd like to be sure I have the support of the strongest lungs in all of England. "Ah!" I hear you say. "It's all very well for you to expect me to go on a recruiting drive for this splendid Section of yours. But suppose they ask me what else there is besides honour and glory?" Well, Mother, apart from belonging to the smartest unit in the Army the pay is very generous. You get a half-penny for every festive balloon you inflate and a full two-pence for every balloon sculpture created. On top of this, food, clothing and accommodation are thrown in free of charge!

So tell those who are interested to go down to the London Rubber Company and see Major Jurecks. Tell them to rally round! Maybe old Harry and his chums will be interested. After all, what is better? A chest filled with medals or enough white feathers to stuff a duvet? Old Jurecks will put them right. And, if any of those chaps have their School Certificates and a bent for science, they may even end up in our top secret Helium Unit. Not only do these boffins produce festive balloons that are lighter than air, they also get the opportunity to talk in silly sounding voices! Now, Mother, what more could a patriotic Englishman ask for?

Your Loving Son,
Horace Scholar"

My mother told me not to take the letter too seriously because my great uncle's service had been blown out of proportion.

Posted by Alfred Scholar NUT TA

REPORT ON THE VISIT BY DR WINTERGREEN AND PROFESSOR NUGGETS

Last Thursday Nuggets and Wintergreen arrived for a demonstration of the school time machine. I offered our two eminent guests a glass of Gooseberry Wine which they accepted. It was comforting to know that like we headmasters, psychiatrists and physicists also drank on duty. However, whilst they regarded it as a simple source of refreshment, to us it was a necessity. Whilst the professor was examining the machine I asked Dr Wintergreen if there was any particular period of history he'd like to go to. The doctor laughed and said that if this was a *genuine* time machine then he'd like to go to ancient Greece. This was where the first crude brain operations were carried out using something called trepanning. He explained that the operation involved drilling a hole in the head in order to relieve pressure. I jokingly replied that the first brain surgeons must have been carpenters and wondered if they French polished the skull and fitted a handle to it. Nuggets didn't seem amused. He said the only joke was our time machine and he was looking forward to unmasking me as a charlatan. I told him I wasn't a Charlatan, my name was Scholar. The Charlatans, who were from Burton-on-Trent, were distantly related to us on my mother's side. This appeared to stump him somewhat.

The two of them then entered the time machine. Whereupon I set the dates and turned the contraption on. I didn't go with them because I had to count last week's takings. On their return they were unable to speak for several minutes. Finally Wintergreen told me that he hadn't believed that this was a genuine time machine. He'd been assured by Nuggets that he and many of his fellow physicists considered time travel to be impossible. And, even it wasn't, given our present scientific knowledge this level of technology just didn't exist.

Yet, 20 minutes ago, Wintergreen said he'd conversed with Hippocrates himself who had demonstrated the operation on a man who just happened to be passing by. Unfortunately the man died. Wintergreen told me he pointed out that operating on someone just to demonstrate a procedure was highly unethical. What about the Hippocratic Oath that a doctor should do no harm? He's clearly harmed that man. Hippocrates had just laughed and told Wintergreen not to believe everything he read.

As for Nuggets? He'd been rendered totally speechless and is now undergoing intensive therapy along with Oliver Cromwell. Wintergreen has assured me that he'll confirm our time machine is the totally genuine article. We now have confirmation from a psychiatrist. A man trained to distinguish fantasy from reality. And, if the physicist ever manages to regain his marbles, he'll also confirm that the time machine is kosher. My wife has promised to do her best in bringing Nuggets back to some sort of sanity. But even she can't work miracles. At least not every time. With Wintergreen's absolutely compelling testimony to the veracity of our time machine we can finally begin producing them in bulk amounts. Creating not only more wealth for your beloved Headmaster, but more prestige. The Nobel Prize beckons!

Posted by Alfred Scholar NUT TA

RE: REPORT ON THE VISIT BY NUGGETS AND WINTERGREEN

Don't count your Nobel Prizes until they've been hatched! A relative of mine runs a forensic laboratory down in Kent and I've sent him a sample of your gooseberry wine. It'll be interesting to see what he makes of it.

Posted by Malakas God of Bloggers

MESSAGE FOR MALAKAS

Young Wheek has assured me that you can send this monkey's uncle of yours a gallon of the blooming stuff and he won't find anything untoward in it!

Posted by Alfred Scholar NUT TA

Malakas could bluster all he liked. I wasn't in the slightest bit worried because I knew that our science department along with the school distillery which produces the refreshing beverage called "Wheek's Gooseberry Wine, operates to standards well above those required by Government Health & Safety Regulations. Indeed, let me quote what the web based "International Peruvian Institute of Global Safety" have to say about both places. "Having received payment for our services we are happy to confirm that the Wallygrange Grammar School Science Department and Distillery are, without any doubt whatsoever, the safest places on earth!" It is this - along with some other things - that allow me to sleep peacefully at night.

SOME SAD NEWS

I've been told that the parents of one of our Year 8 pupils have finally decided to turn off their son's life support. This followed a day of gut wrenching contemplation. During which one can only imagine just how hard their guts were wrenched. On the plus side they have accepted medical opinion and finally realised that the hospital was running up an electricity bill for no good reason. Common sense eventually prevailed. This boy's accident in the chemistry lab is a sober reminder that pupils must remember the difference between a "flammable" compound and an "inflammable" one. This has been a hard lesson but, as I'm regularly wont to say, the harder the lesson the more chance that it will sink in. After all, you can't make an omelette without breaking some eggs. And I'm sure we all hope sincerely that George has ended up in an *in*flammable destination. But no, you're right; we really shouldn't joke about this.

Posted by Alfred Scholar NUT TA

WHAT'S THIS? SURELY NOT ANOTHER FIRST CLASS BOOK FOR THE ENGLISH GCSE SYLLABUS! OUR CUP RUNNETH OVER!

The Anderson family suffer from an obsessive-compulsive disorder that makes them loathe to leave *anything* behind when they go on holiday. So they pack as much as they can. And *then* some! As a result their luggage is so heavy it's the only thing the plane can carry - and then only if the aircraft is refuelled in flight! An easy task for the RAF, but more difficult for a commercial airline. The book is full to the brim with white knuckle mishaps like collapsing taxis, hotel floors and hernias. You'll laugh your socks off – but you'd better leave them behind because there's no room for them in their luggage!

Posted by Alfred Scholar NUT TA

BUDDING GYNAECOLOGISTS?

Year 9 have just completed their latest project in metalwork. This project had a medical theme and involved making duckbill pattern stainless steel vaginal and anal speculums. To test them the pupils have taken them home and will ask their mothers to try them out.

Posted by Alfred Scholar NUT TA

A WARNING ABOUT THE VAGINAL SPECULUMS!

One pupil, Roger Billings, has reported that his mother was taken to hospital when she and her husband were unable to get the speculum out of her vagina.

Posted by Alfred Scholar NUT TA

RE: WARNING ABOUT THE VAGINAL SPECULUMS!

Is this a product recall? You'll be on "Watchdog" next.

Posted by Malakas God of Bloggers

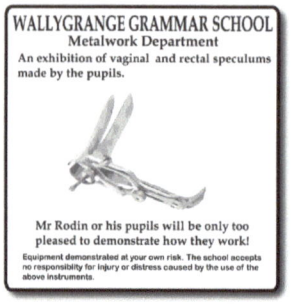

JOINING THE ARMY!

Yesterday I had a letter from the Ministry of Defence. At first I thought they'd changed their minds and decide to court martial me. But they've clearly decided that the accounting error at Aldershot is money under the bridge. Instead, they expressed the rather vain hope that some of our pupils would consider enlisting in the British Army. Well, they're hardly likely to enlist in the French one. Unless they like eating snails and surrendering to the Germans. I told the MOD that if they couldn't recruit any Wallygrangians in the First and Second World War, they haven't much chance now. I reminded them that even with conscription they'd singularly failed to get even *one* recruit from Wallygrange. It seems everyone was declared either physically or mentally unfit. And that included the staff! And I told them that the situation here hasn't changed one iota. Wallygrange does not, and never has, produced warriors of any size or shape whatsoever.

I told the MOD that Wallygrange, for humanitarian reasons, teaches pacifism. However, I added the rider that our humanitarian beliefs don't stretch to humanity itself. Just to us. We consider ourselves to be like the Quakers. The very thought of physical violence makes us quake.

Posted by Alfred Scholar NUT TA.

THE ENGLISH GCSE SYLLABUS GAINS YET ANOTHER BOOK!

As a sop to the British Army, (and may they long continue to lay down their lives to protect us pacifists), I wrote this book over the weekend. It's about as true story as I could make it and it's about the Secretary of the Scunthorpe International Nudist Society who joined the British army in WW2. Unwilling to wear any form of clothing he was given a Royal Warrant by King George, (himself a closet naturalist – which is a bit of a misnomer because closets can contain clothes), to fight Hitler naked. Now that *would* have been a sight! Especially if this had been a *WWE* cage fight with both men in their birthday suits! But we must return to reality and dispense with these flights of fancy which are the natural side effects of imbibing Wheek Gooseberry Wine. Against all the odds, given that the Germans were more than eager to shoot at his naughty bits, Bert survived the war only to be killed when he was trampled after falling into the Elephant Enclosure at Chester Zoo in 1952.

Apart from improving the pupil's knowledge of fine literature the book may encourage some of them to join the colours. Especially those pupils in Mr Honeybee's Naturist Club. The book is available from Scholar Publishing at the meagre price of £65. 99 + VAT

Posted by Alfred Scholar NUT TA.

BEAU JEST?

The Senior Caretaker tells me he was in the Foreign Legion before he joined the SAS. And he loved eating snails. He told me that in the Legion snails are eaten in a special way. Each man kneels by the side of the table with his mouth open. And the snails have to crawl into it and are eaten alive. I jokingly asked him if there'd been many cases of shellshock.

Posted by Alfred Scholar, NUT TA

YES! THE GCSE ENGLISH SYLLABUS WELCOMES YET *ANOTHER* BOOK TO ITS FOLD!

I refer to "Mutiny!" by C. Mann. We've probably all heard of the Mutiny of the Bounty. (And, no, it wasn't about people who refused to eat that popular chocolate bar filled with coconut. I checked with the History Master). He also told me that ever since Jack Tar set out to sea in Hearts of Oak, there have been mutinies. They come with the job. As did being virtually paralytic after a surfeit of 200% rum, a flagon of which was passed out every hour. The history teacher went on to tell me that back in the old days old salts were frequently lashed until skinless by the cat of nine tails or, if the cat wasn't available, by the dog of nine legs. This cruel and almost inhuman punishment was served out almost daily and for the most trivial of infractions. Like smoking in the powder room. But even this failed to quell the unruly sailor's love of taking control of the ship. After all, who can live knee deep in bilge water eating weevil encrusted biscuits so tough they'd have broken King Neptune's teeth! Knowing full well that your foppish officers dined in style in their wardroom furnished by the best Chippendale could nail together? That's what the history teacher told me. Or that's what I thought he'd said. Set in Elizabethan times, this remarkable book tells the story of the Royal Navy frigate, Warspite. Whereas Captain Bligh ruled with an iron rod, Captain Alf Asleep ruled with a feather mattress! Flat on his back, this man came into the navy with his eyes closed and hasn't opened them since. He's a dreamer. And, when the crew decided to mutiny, it was a wakeup call to the captain!

Posted by Alfred Scholar, NUT TA

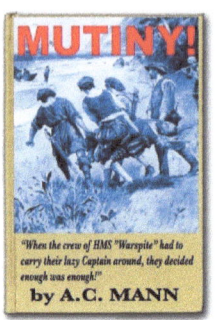

(Available from Scholar Publishing at the meagre price of £65. 99 + VAT & P&P)

Cleanliness is also something we're pretty keen on here at Wallygrange. Not too keen otherwise the staff and pupils would be spending all day taking a shower or washing their hands. So the school policy is to allow a certain amount of grime on each individual. Good honest work often produces good honest dirt! That's what I think my father told me when I visited him in Strangeways Prison. How was he to know that fraud was illegal? He wasn't a solicitor. The judge was well out of order telling him that ignorance was no excuse in the law. Balderdash! The world is full of ignorant people! If that judge were to show you a street map of Paris and point to any of the streets, could you tell him the names of the people who live there? I'll bet you couldn't. In which case you'd be in prison! The law's as ass and that's all there is to it. Fortunately my mother took over running the school in his enforced absence. I'm telling you this to show that I and my family are only human with all – or at least quite a few – of the vices humans are prone to.

WASHDAY BLUES!

I've had an irate Mrs Netherspoon complaining that her son came home yesterday with a load of congealed blood and guts smeared all over his uniform. Her son had informed her that it was due to a scientific experiment and I was happily able to confirm that her son was, on this occasion at least, telling the full truth. The Science Teacher was demonstrating what would happen if someone inserted – accidentally or on purpose – a high pressure air hose into their anus. To demonstrate the teacher used a compressor and a dead pig. The air blew the carcass up like a balloon until it exploded, covering us all in the dead pig's innards! It's humbling when one witnesses the discomfort we sometimes suffer in order to enrich our scientific knowledge.

Posted by Alfred Scholar, NUT TA

The blog took on a decidedly culinary flavour when we discovered a pastry based gastronomic delight...

WHO ATE ALL THE PIES?

On Tuesday I presented the school with some meat pies I'd discovered on a trip to Victorian London in the school time machine. The pies proved to be extremely delicious. In fact we've decided to order some more from this bakery.

Posted by Alfred Scholar NUT TA

RE: WHO ATE ALL THE PIES?

A delivery of pies from Mrs Lovett's Bakery in London arrived this morning and went down like hot cakes, (well, more like hot pies). The School Cook said she'd never seen food go down that fast. The pupils were clamouring for seconds! This was good news because I made quite a tidy profit on those pies. Given that Mrs Lovett charged only an old Penny for each one! As a result, I've placed a regular order with the bakery. Not only will they be supplying the school kitchen, the pies will also be on sale to the staff.

Posted by Alfred Scholar NUT TA

OUR FOOD TECHNOLOGY DEPARTMENT

This will be the department's second year and I must thank the staff and pupils for all the hard work they've put into it. I'd mention their names but, let's be honest, there are so many staff and pupils I can't be expected to remember *all* their names. Come on! I'm not that much of a genius! Anyway, their theme that "Everything can be deep fried in fat" has proved to be a huge success. The only dissenting voices have come from the NHS and the Heart Foundation. What do these people know about teaching children? They should stick to minding their own business.

The department is proud to announce a sponsorship deal with Hartstop's Lard Company of Newcastle and new school year promises to be an exciting one for Food Technology. Especially with the arrival of an extra *deep* fat fryer donated by Hartstop. So deep you need a submersible to see the bottom. Only joking! What does this mean? Well, the staff tell me its means that food can now be fried at a depth of 50 feet. Of course, this means more lard. But more lard means more taste.

Posted by Alfred Scholar NUT TA

THOSE PIES

Do the pupils know that London bakery that's supplying the school with pies has a connection to Sweeny Todd's barber shop? And that the owner, Mrs Lovett, has been accused of encouraging cannibalism.

Posted by Malakas God of Bloggers

BEWARE OF TROLLS!

Let's just forget about pies, shall we? The staff, pupils and parents are not interested in some sort of Great British Bake Off. They want to know who *you* are, Mr Malakas! Because I think you're a troll.

Posted by Alfred Scholar NUT TA

BEWARE OF MRS LOVETT'S PIES!

Don't try to change the subject! Is it true the 6th Form science department found human DNA in those pies? Yes or no?

Posted by Malakas God of Bloggers

BEWARE OF TROLLS!

I'm not trying to change the subject...you are! I want to talk about you and you keep harping on about some pies. Who are you, Malakas?

Posted by Alfred Scholar NUT TA

BEWARE OF MRS LOVETT'S PIES!

I am your worst nightmare.

Posted by Malakas God of Bloggers

BEWARE OF TROLLS!

I hope not. I've had some real humdingers – especially after an Undertaker's Lunch. It's like a Ploughman's Lunch but the cheese and bread are mouldy and it's washed down with a pint of Wheek Gooseberry Wine.

Posted by Alfred Scholar NUT TA

MEAT IS JUST MEAT!

Yesterday I paid a visit to Mrs Lovett who has been providing our school with a selection of pies and sausage rolls. She's admitted that the delicious filling in the pies and sausage rolls does contain *some* human meat. But only about 94%. Even so I was a little shocked. The Wallygrange Grammar School has an enviable reputation to uphold. Alright, it wasn't 100% human meat but if the tabloids thought we were in any way involved in cannibalism they'd have a field day. Although the liberal broadsheets, like "The Guardian" would defend our right to eat what we bally well like! And more power to their elbow! As a solicitor, I think the fact that the meat is human, like us, means we have a human right to eat it. Although I've yet to test that in court.

Mrs Lovett told me not to worry. In olden days barbers also performed surgery and, as luck would have it, her fiancé was himself a local barber. In fact, he was one of the last barbers in the world to perform surgical operations. So that the meat came from amputated limbs and defunct internal organs that would otherwise have been incinerated. I must tell you it was a great relief to hear that no one had been killed to titillate our taste buds. Not like those missionaries who ended up in the pot. That would have been in bad taste, if you'll excuse the pun. Had I been forced to cancel our regular order there would probably have been a riot. Staff and pupils just can't get enough of those pies. So now we can relax and joke that our food does cost an arm and a leg!

Posted by Alfred Scholar NUT TA

Whilst peace of mind had been restored on the catering front, the item below was a salutary reminder that the streets outside the school could sometimes be less than peaceful.

RE: THE RECENT INCIDENT OUTSIDE THE SCHOOL GATES

About the incident when one of our pupils was dragged into a car whilst on his way home yesterday. This has been explained by the police who said they knew all about it. He was actually being arrested.

Posted by Alfred Scholar NUT TA.

A MUSICAL NOTE

Hey! You scallywag! Is it true the school orchestra are practicing a song you've written about me called, "Let's kick old Malakas in his nackers." I assume my "nackers" are those two things that hang between my legs.
Posted by Malakas God of Bloggers

RE: A MUSICAL NOTE
Correct! I called them that because "bollocks" doesn't rhyme with "Malakas." This was just a little ditty I came up with in the bathroom whilst shaving. It's a shame Frank Sinatra has kicked the bucket. This would have been perfect for a warbler like him.
Posted by Alfred Scholar NUT TA

RE: A MUSICAL NOTE
You'll be singing a different tune when I've finished with you!
Posted by Malakas God of Bloggers

RE: A MUSICAL NOTE
I've heard ducks fart. You don't scare me, Malakas!
Posted by Alfred Scholar NU TA.

A REPORT ON WHEEK GOOSEBERRY WINE!
Not scared, eh? I thought you might be interested in this. It's from that relative of mine who tested the sample of Gooseberry Wine I sent her.

"You sent me a one litre bottle containing Wheek Gooseberry Wine and you asked me to analyze it. This I have done.

Your note that accompanied the sample explained that the distillation process used in producing WGW is similar to that used in homeopathy. As you know, homeopathy involves diluting a substance until not one atom of the stuff remains. So I wasn't surprised when a chemical analysis revealed that the sample you sent contained nothing but pure water. And, if it wasn't for the fact that the water in the bottle had a distinct smell of gooseberries, I'd have been sure this was one of your wind ups. Not only that, it smelt as though these gooseberries had been marinated in a strong alcohol. Needless to say this should have been impossible given the fact that the bottle contained no trace of either of the two substances.

So I decided to taste it. Sure enough, it also tasted of gooseberries. And the alcohol was quite strong. Because there was no trace of alcohol in the sample I had to guess the volume and I'd say it was about 30/35%. It was also rather nice and I'm afraid to say I finished the bottle. What happened next defies all rational explanation. The laboratory seemed to spin and I momentarily blacked out. When I came round I was in church wearing a wedding dress that had been smeared in what looked like beeswax and I was about to get married to a stuffed gorilla wearing a top hat. The service itself was being conducted by a Greek Archbishop whilst a Salvation Army Band played, "Whilst the Saints Came Marching In."

You can imagine my horror! When I tried to protest the Archbishop slapped me across the face and told me that God had ordered this wedding and I was not to stand in the way of true love. I then decided to make a run for it and Archbishop tried to stop me. But, because I was coated in beeswax, I slipped out of his grasp. Unfortunately the beeswax was my undoing because someone tripped me up and I slid down the aisle at top speed, hitting the church door and knocking myself out cold.

When I came round I was lying in bed naked with the stuffed gorilla lying on top of me. The Archbishop and the brass band were also there. According to the Archbishop they had come to make sure the marriage was consummated! Fortunately at this point I blacked out again. When I came round I was back in the laboratory. However, because I'd conducted the test you wanted whilst I was alone no one had been there to see what had happened. I can only conclude that this Wheek Gooseberry Wine contains some sort of hallucinogenic compound. But it's impossible to determine just what this compound is."

It's a shame she drank it all and there were no witnesses. I'll just have to get some more samples and send them to New Scotland Yard. Then the poo-poo will really hit the fan and you can say goodbye to Wallygrange School! I hope you like porridge, Alfred. Because after giving children a hallucinogenic substance you'll be eating a lot of it at one of HM's Establishments!

Posted by Malakas God of Bloggers

MY VISIT TO LONDON

Great news!

On Thursday I went down to London to visit the Prime Minister and members the Cabinet at No. 10. The invitation came after I sent them some Wheek Gooseberry Wine in the hope that we might be able to export it. The PM has been banging on about reducing the national debt so schemes like this for increasing exports can only help. I told them the audacious and often colourful history of Wheek Gooseberry Wine and its connection with Wallygrange Grammar School. I also mentioned the atomic toilets and the time machine. They seemed suitably impressed so I was hoping for good things. And it looks like my hopes have come true. The PM just emailed me. He'd sent a few bottles to the Governors of the Bank of England and told them about my plan to export Wheek Gooseberry Wine. The Governors were so impressed they voted unanimously to do some quantitative easing to give our school a hefty injection of cash. Some of this will be used to expand the distillery in order to meet future demand.

Posted by Alfred Scholar NUT TA

A FINAL WORD FROM THE GREAT MALAKAS...

There must be millions of blogs on the Internet. Written by millions of sad mortals. There are sad geeks masturbating over their latest bit of hi-tech equipment or some arcane piece of code. And even sadder mortals boring everyone to death with the minutia of their totally empty lives. Even 90 year old flatulents are blogging. Thankfully, they won't be doing it for long. The Grim Reaper will see to that.

And that's where I come in. As the Great Malakas, God of Bloggers I have made it my solemn duty to examine each blog on the Internet. For I am also the God of the All Seeing

Eye. This magical eye once belonged to the Freemasons but now it serves the Great Malakas! Those blogs that do not meet my demanding standards are deleted. My decisions are final.

Today I have deleted 453 blogs.

And this has been one of them...

THE END